"Years ago a friend said to me, 'The only [...] Lord is wishing you had.' Most of us, in v[...] But all of us will wait, and we will wait on God. His [...] sync with ours. What do we do while we wait? Mark Vroegop tea[...] waiting on God is living on what we know to be true about God when we don't know what is true about our life. Thank you, Mark, for sharing with us how and why to wait and doing so in such a clear, biblical, transferable way. What a treasure!"

Crawford W. Lorritts Jr., speaker; radio host; author; Founder and President, Beyond Our Generation

"*Waiting Isn't a Waste* is full of timely and practical encouragement for every reader. Instead of trying to avoid waiting at all costs, this book will help you embrace it as a good gift from God."

Ruth Chou Simons, *Wall Street Journal* bestselling author; artist; Founder, GraceLaced

"Waiting is one of the most difficult parts of life, yet also the most common. Most of life involves waiting. The speed of modern life tempts us to view all waiting as a waste. Mark Vroegop helps us develop a biblical framework for waiting on God, inviting us to see times of waiting as opportunities for worship and growth. Viewed rightly, waiting provides pathways to contentment and calmness—a healthy, nonpressured embracing of life as God intended it. This timely, readable book will be edifying to everyone who reads it."

Gavin Ortlund, President, Truth Unites; Theologian-in-Residence, Immanuel Church, Nashville, Tennessee

"Waiting fills the gap between our current reality and our unrealized expectations. While we may feel stuck, forgotten, disappointed, and confused, Mark Vroegop's new book *Waiting Isn't a Waste* faithfully reminds us that God is purposefully at work in transformative ways. This book is a helpful and needed encouragement to live in the truth of what we know about God when we don't understand his plan for our lives."

Melissa B. Kruger, author; Vice President of Discipleship Programming, The Gospel Coalition

"I had no idea the Bible said so much about waiting. As someone with a terrible reputation for being impatient, this is not surprising. This book is a godsend to me and others in our day. How desperately we need to hear the biblical and practical wisdom it contains."

Daniel L. Akin, President, Southeastern Baptist Theological Seminary

"This is an important book for all of us who think that waiting is unproductive and annoying. Whether in the doctor's waiting room or at a red light or, worse yet, in a life crisis that makes us vulnerable to the dark riders of fear, anxiety, and doubt, waiting is rarely thought of as a friend. Thankfully, Mark Vroegop has given us a fresh biblical perspective that radically changes our view of waiting. With practical steps forged through his own experience, Vroegop leads us into a new appreciation for the 'waits' of life as we place our trust in our God who is at work for our good and his glory when our lives seem stuck on pause."

Joe Stowell, Bible teacher; special assistant to the President, Moody Bible Institute

"It is hard to think of a less requested yet more urgently needed project than a rehabilitation of our practical theology of waiting. Packed with insight into the intersection of waiting and hope, waiting and intentionality, waiting and the trustworthiness of God, waiting and building enduring Christian community, this book is laden with distillations of Scripture that I sincerely pray will change how you and I live every day for the rest of our lives."

J. Alasdair Groves, Executive Director, Christian Counseling & Educational Foundation; coauthor, *Untangling Emotions*

"I stink at waiting. I really do. In recent days, I have been reminded of this. This is why I was thankful to know this rare, timely book had been written. *Waiting Isn't a Waste* was exactly what I needed to press against my impatience and remind me how much waiting is a part of God's good plan for all of us. Everything Mark Vroegop writes is clear, biblical, practical, and thoughtful, and this book is no exception. Whether you are a pastor, church member, or simply someone looking for hope in the waiting, this book is definitely for you. I know of nothing like it."

Brian Croft, Executive Director, Practical Shepherding

"With Mark Vroegop as your guide, learning to wait can be one of the greatest journeys you will embark on. He invites us to see what we experience as annoyances and long seasons of anxiety as opportunities to discover who God is and his tender care of us. Vroegop does not ask us to ignore the challenges of waiting or trivialize the anxiety we feel. Instead, *Waiting Isn't a Waste* encourages us to embrace waiting because when we do, we will find ourselves on the path to flourishing."

Darby Strickland, Faculty and Counselor, Christian Counseling & Educational Foundation; author, *Is It Abuse?*

"In this personal and profound volume, Mark Vroegop points us toward redemption in the waiting of life. With practical advice, theological clarity, and personal warmth, Vroegop presents waiting as a transformational discipline of the Christian life, something that brings peace into our lives through a deeper connection to the Lord. For our generation that is always impatient and ruthlessly driven, this book is a manifesto for the countercultural calling of authentic Christian discipleship."

D. Michael Lindsay, President, Taylor University

Waiting Isn't a Waste

Waiting Isn't a Waste

*The Surprising Comfort of Trusting God
in the Uncertainties of Life*

Mark Vroegop

Foreword by Jen Wilkin

WHEATON, ILLINOIS

Trade paperback ISBN: 978-1-4335-9097-9
ePub ISBN: 978-1-4335-9099-3
PDF ISBN: 978-1-4335-9098-6

Library of Congress Cataloging-in-Publication Data

Names: Vroegop, Mark, 1971– author.
Title: Waiting isn't a waste : the surprising comfort of trusting God in the uncertainties of life / Mark Vroegop.
Description: Wheaton, Illinois : Crossway, [2024] | Includes bibliographical references and index.
Identifiers: LCCN 2023039211 (print) | LCCN 2023039212 (ebook) | ISBN 9781433590979 (trade paperback) | ISBN 9781433590986 (pdf) | ISBN 9781433590993 (epub)
Subjects: LCSH: Trust in God—Christianity. | Waiting (Philosophy)
Classification: LCC BV4637 .V76 2024 (print) | LCC BV4637 (ebook) | DDC 234/.2—dc23/eng/20231229
LC record available at https://lccn.loc.gov/2023039211
LC ebook record available at https://lccn.loc.gov/2023039212

Crossway is a publishing ministry of Good News Publishers.

VP		33	32	31	30	29	28	27	26	25	24
15	14	13	12	11	10	9	8	7	6	5	4	3	2	1

To Dale Shaw:

"Those who wait upon GOD *get fresh strength. . . .*
They run and don't get tired,
They walk and don't lag behind."

ISAIAH 40:31 (MSG)

Thanks for waiting!

Contents

Foreword

AS I WRITE THESE WORDS, I am waiting. I would imagine you are too. I'm waiting for a child to return from a very long stay overseas, for a friend to get her pathology reports, for a family member to come to faith, and for several forms of grief to subside. I'm also waiting for a repairman who is three days late. And I'm waiting for the heat of an infernal Texas summer to finally give way to the first cold front of fall. I'm experiencing varying levels of success with each of these waits, and not all of my responses to them would make me a candidate for sainthood.

We owe an immeasurable debt to the great theologian Tom Petty for saying what we all feel: the waiting is the hardest part.[1] If ever a truer lyric were set to music, I am unaware of it. And we're not good at it. In fact, we are worse at it than we were when Petty's song was racing up the charts in 1981. Research shows that the average attention span has shrunk from twelve seconds in the year 2000 to eight seconds in 2015. This means our attention span is now officially shorter than that of a goldfish by a full second.[2]

---

1. Tom Petty, "The Waiting," track 1, *Hard Promises* (Universal City, CA: Backstreet, 1981).
2. John Stevens, "Decreasing Attention Spans and Your Website, Social Media Strategy," *Adweek*, June 7, 2016, https://adweek.com.

We live in a culture of instant gratification, where streaming services deliver our entertainment in seconds, Amazon delivers our packages the same day, and Google answers our questions instantly. Our commute is kept as wait-free as possible by apps that route and reroute according to traffic patterns. And we never endure the nerve-wracking wait of getting lost on the way to our destination. In other words, we live in a culture that doesn't just cater to goldfish; it produces them. Waiting is seen as an evil to eliminate instead of as a virtue to cultivate. And because waiting is seen as the enemy, our anger and frustration flare when our expected timetables are not met.

But here is good news for the Christ follower: if you've been looking for a simple way to shine like a star in a crooked genera-tion, cultivate the virtue of patience in waiting. Admittedly, that is much easier said than done. It's one thing to wait for your coffee drink in a drive-through, and it's quite another to wait for an illness to resolve or a long-overdue apology to be spoken. The sheer number of hard waits we will face in our lifetimes presents both the challenge and the opportunity of growing in virtue, of growing in Christlikeness.

Impatience is all well and good for the unbeliever, but the Christian faith is, by definition, one of delayed gratification. The children of God are, and always have been, called upon to wait. We wait for God's kingdom to come in fullness, but our waiting is distinctly different from that of the unbeliever. No white-knuckled, jaw-clenched waiting will do for those whose hope is anchored in the bedrock of the finished work of Christ. The enthusiastic expres-sion "I can't wait!" is captured in the maranatha cry of Revelation 22:20, but heaven help us if the citizens of the kingdom of heaven quite literally cannot wait during this life. Patience is the fourth virtue listed in the fruit of the Spirit. If we are progressively being sanctified, we should expect to see it grow in our lives.

That's why the book you are holding matters. Mark Vroegop wants to help you to wait like a Christian. He wants to sit with you in your waiting and show you how to endure by practicing time-tested and biblical disciplines. But more than that, he wants you to know that *waiting is itself a help*. We have much to learn from plotlines that are slow to resolve, from dissonance that settles in like dense fog, from circumstances that take longer than we expect and ask more than we can bear. Mark's voice is the voice of a friend and fellow sojourner, calling us to wait well.

The famous seventeenth-century English poet and statesman John Milton lost his sight at the age of forty-two. A man of deep faith and action, he wrestled with his new limit and with the permanent losses it marked. In the first seasons of his blindness, he wrote Sonnet 19, reflecting on his physical inability to serve God as he had, having taken up the yoke of darkness. He notes, "[those] who best bear his mild yoke, they serve him best." He recognizes that his blindness might yet have purpose, with his heart-stopping final line: "They also serve who only stand and wait." Ten years later, born from the darkness of waiting, he would publish his greatest work, *Paradise Lost*.

Waiting does not preclude serving the Lord. It just reshapes it. May you find in these pages, as I have, strength and wisdom for the waitings you are ordained to wait. Be they great or small, may God be glorified in your fruitful patience and steadfastness.

Jen Wilkin

Introduction

Wasting Our Waiting

They who wait for the Lᴏʀᴅ shall renew
their strength;
they shall mount up with wings like eagles;
they shall run and not be weary;
they shall walk and not faint.

ISAIAH 40:31

THIS BOOK IS ABOUT the "gaps of life" and how the Bible calls us to fill the void of uncertainty by waiting on God.

That's not a new concept.

Waiting on God is an ancient idea found throughout the Bible. However, it's easy to ignore or dismiss. We might be tempted to write off waiting on God as "old school" or as a spiritual theme relegated to an era of history where Christians seemed a bit too serious. What's more, most of us don't enjoy waiting for anything. As a result, we tend to view the gaps of life as something—at best— to be tolerated. Add some stress or pain or time into the mix, and

1

you probably know what happens. Rather than worshiping our way through uncertainty and experiencing peace, our tendency is to fill the gaps of life with fear, anxiety, frustration, or anger.

For most of us, waiting feels like a waste.

I've been there. I *am* there.

That's why I've written this book.

Confessions of an Impatient Multitasker

Some books are written out of personal expertise. Not this one! I wrote this book because I see a need in myself and in those around me. In full disclosure, not only am I terrible at waiting, but it seems I have a natural bias against it. "Doesn't everyone?" you might ask. That's probably true at some level. But when I say I'm bad at waiting, I mean it. It's been a problem for a long time.

Let's start with my last name. Good luck trying to pronounce it, although it's much easier than you'd think. Vroegop is Dutch. What you probably don't know is that most Dutch last names mean something practical. That's because in the 1800s Napoleon required my forefathers to select a last name. Other families chose names associated with their work: Shoemaker (shoe maker), Bakker (baker), or Meijer (steward). Others identified their kin by a location: Vander Meer (from the lake), Boogaard (from the orchard), or Vander Molen (from the mill). What about my last name? Vroegop literally means "early up." To this day it makes me smirk. You see, when my great-great-great-grandparents considered what we would name ourselves, they made a statement about how early we get out of bed. They could have chosen *napper*, *slow*, *Sabbath keeper*, or *loves sleep*. Nope. My last name and its meaning creates an identity: "Mark Early Up." As a child, I remember my family valuing rising early, being productive, and personal discipline. My mom used to say, "Work hard. Play hard." This mindset is part of who I am.

Not waiting is literally in my last name.

My personality doesn't help either. I'm decidedly pro-action. I love to work and accomplish things. I like to do things in the right way and fix what's broken. If you are into personality tests, you might not be surprised to learn that I have the Activator talent on Strengths Finder, and I'm probably an Enneagram 1. Based upon the DISC test, I like to see results. A great day off for me is a to-do list with lots of completed tasks. Getting things done energizes me, and I've read a lot of books about productivity. When I attended a Franklin Planner seminar thirty years ago, I was captivated with making the best use of "discretionary time." In my first professional job, I'll never forget when a vice president at a Christian college commended me for bringing work to do while I waited for an appointment with him to begin. I'm pretty sure that sitting quietly, daydreaming, or engaging his secretary in small talk would not have been recognized. I learned quickly that multitasking and working hard were rewarded. They made me feel affirmed.

Unfortunately, pastoral ministry and theological education made my aversion for waiting worse. I gravitated toward verses about life stewardship ("To whom much was given, of him much will be required," Luke 12:48) and redeeming the time (" . . . making the best use of the time, because the days are evil," Eph. 5:16). The endless demands of ministry created a spiritualized "fifth gear" in my drive. When I learned that a respected leader or a Puritan slept only four hours a day, I found another justification for passionate activity. Upon reading *Don't Waste Your Life* by John Piper,

I deeply resonated with the theological vision of living passionately for the glory of God. I was determined not to waste my life.

But in the process of not wasting my life, I wasted something else: my waiting.

The last few years surfaced a deep deficiency in how I think about and practice waiting on God. The global pandemic that we thought would last a few months dragged on for two years. Cultural divisions and church controversies created countless no-win decisions. I can't remember a time when I was more aware of the massive gaps in life. I felt powerless all the time. When my old patterns of overworking, overthinking, and overplanning didn't work, I found myself filling this canyon of uncertainty with anxiety, fear, and frustration. While I knew how to lament the grief I felt, I didn't know how to wait on the Lord with this massive tension.

I needed to stop wasting my waiting.

I still do.

The Aim of This Book

I wish this journey was complete, but it feels like it's just begun. I've got a long way to go. There are a lot of gaps to consider. Life is full of uncertainty. I expect you agree. In fact, you may have picked up this book because you're in a season of waiting. Perhaps it relates to your career, singleness, marriage, pregnancy, health, relationships, or some conflict. The list could be even longer because we're always waiting. Maybe you've noticed a higher degree of simmering frustration, pervasive anxiety, low-grade anger, or a concerning cynicism in your life, and you'd like to change. Perhaps you sense that waiting isn't a strength, and you're curious about how to grow in this area. Or God may be preparing you for a season that's around the corner, and this book is one way to get you ready. Regardless of the circumstances, I'm glad you're considering this topic.

Everyone waits.

I don't think we do it very well.

The aim of this book is to help us take steps in learning to wait. My goal is to unpack this definition: *Waiting on God is living on what I know to be true about God when I don't know what's true about my life.* And I hope that by the time you are finished, you'll no longer waste your waiting; I hope you'll see waiting as redemptive, something helpful.

How Do We Wait?

This book assumes that we will wait. The question is: How can we learn to wait on God in a way that leads to transformation and peace?

As we'll see along this journey together, waiting is a theme throughout the Old and New Testaments. Probably the most well-known verses are found in Isaiah 40. They're promises given to God's people as they faced national uncertainty and personal pain. Israel wondered if God had forgotten them and if there was no hope in things turning around. Isaiah reminds them about who God is and then offers the promise of renewed strength:

Why do you say, O Jacob,
    and speak, O Israel,
"My way is hidden from the LORD,
    and my right is disregarded by my God"?
Have you not known? Have you not heard?
The LORD is the everlasting God,
    the Creator of the ends of the earth.

He does not faint or grow weary;
 his understanding is unsearchable.
He gives power to the faint,
 and to him who has no might he increases strength.
Even youths shall faint and be weary,
 and young men shall fall exhausted;
but they who wait for the LORD shall renew their strength;
 they shall mount up with wings like eagles;
they shall run and not be weary;
 they shall walk and not faint. (Isa. 40:27–31)

That's an amazing promise! I want to understand and embrace this biblical vision. I yearn for the kind of power, strength, and perseverance that's promised in this text. Don't you? I'm tired of wasting my waiting. Aren't you? I want to learn how to wait on God.

If you look ahead, our path is marked out by six chapters. I've chosen a characteristic for each one because the issue isn't *if* we wait, but *how* we wait.

So, how do we wait on God?

- Honestly: waiting is hard
- Frequently: waiting is common
- Thoughtfully: waiting is biblical
- Patiently: waiting is slow
- Intentionally: waiting is commanded
- Collectively: waiting is relational

Waiting is not just part of our humanity; it's vital to Christianity. That's why the Old and New Testaments talk about it so often. Like many other things, including suffering and the crucifixion, God aims to transform what is painful and confusing. That's also why believers are commanded to wait. From God's perspective, it's good.

But that doesn't mean it's easy.

Life is full of gaps, moments or seasons when we are invited to wait. But if we're not careful and thoughtful, we can fill those gaps with spiritually unhelpful responses. Over the chapters that follow, I hope you'll discover how to fill the gaps of life with what's true about God—to wait on him. What's more, I'll show you a process for worshiping your way through seasons of uncertainty and resisting our typical temptations. I want you to see waiting as more than a delay; our journey will help you (and me) learn the surprising comfort of waiting on God and how it leads to peace.

Waiting isn't a waste.

Let's learn why and how—together.

Reflection Questions

1. What is your disposition and attitude toward waiting?

2. Describe the reasons you picked up this book.

3. What are a few lessons you hope to learn or some questions you want to answer?

4. Describe a season when you waited on the Lord with some measure of spiritual success. How about the opposite?

5. Write out a prayer expressing your desire to learn to wait on the Lord.

1

Honestly

Waiting Is Hard

I am weary with my crying out;
my throat is parched.
My eyes grow dim
with waiting for my God.

PSALM 69:3

LET'S START WITH SOMETHING OBVIOUS: waiting is hard.

You probably picked up this book because you know this to be true. Perhaps you're living through a season where you've been forced to wait, and you're learning how challenging it is. Maybe you started out strong in a time of uncertainty, but you've noticed a nagging sense of anxiety or frustration begin to set in. Whether we consciously know it or not, we have an internal sense of how long things should take. When this is challenged or when our expectations aren't met, we soon discover a rising level of tension.

Waiting is usually a lot harder than we realize—or care to admit.

I think it's safe to say that most people dislike waiting. Do you know anyone who celebrates it? "Oh good, we get to wait." That feels weird or fake, doesn't it? Imagine meeting a friend and asking about her weekend. What would be your immediate response if she said, "I spent three hours waiting on Saturday"? You'd probably groan, right? Waiting feels like a gap in time that's annoying at best and aggravating at worst.

Most of us have a negative bias against it.

Our society makes it worse. In our fast-paced, instant-answer, and quick-results culture, less waiting is a benchmark for success. It's a status symbol. Ever visited Disney World? Purchasing a FastPass affords you the privilege of skipping the line. The next time you visit the counter of a fast-food restaurant, look above the window of the drive-through. You'll probably see a running clock capturing the time to serve each customer. Look closer and you might see a time goal written on a white board. Employees are rewarded for reducing wait times. Airports even started moving baggage claims greater distances from the terminals because customers are willing to walk farther than wait longer at an empty carousel. How many seconds are you willing to wait for a website or video to load before you click somewhere else? Our patience for the "buffering wheel" is decreasing. Efficiency and immediacy are the hallmarks of success in our society. Time is money, right?

Waiting isn't valued in our culture.

This context is important to understand as we learn about the spiritual value of waiting. There's a strong natural assumption, internally and externally, that delays and uncertainty are bad. But as you'll see in the chapters that follow, waiting is commended as something valuable. Waiting is good. What's more, waiting is commanded. Let that sink in.

The Bible commends and commands something that everything in us and everyone around us usually sees as negative.

We've got some work to do.

Waiting Defined

Before we go too far, let's start with a preliminary definition of *waiting* in the Bible. In the Old Testament several Hebrew words are used. In the next chapter, we'll unpack the nuances of different words. But the common thread between them is looking for something or someone with eager expectation.[1] In other words, waiting is a space to be filled. A gap emerges, and we look or hope for something to fill it. From a spiritual standpoint, God fills that gap with himself, his plans, or his promises. Ben Patterson affirms this when he writes, "To wait is to journey in faith toward the things God has promised."[2]

When you find the word *wait* in the Bible, it's important to look for the words it's pointing toward. A few examples:

I waited patiently *for the LORD.* (Ps. 40:1)

My eyes grow dim
with waiting *for my God.* (Ps. 69:3)

1. John E. Hartley, "1994 קָוָה," in *Theological Wordbook of the Old Testament*, ed. R. Laird Harris, Gleason L. Archer Jr., and Bruce K. Waltke (Chicago: Moody, 1999), 791.
2. Ben Patterson, *Waiting: Finding Hope When God Seems Silent* (Downers Grove, IL: InterVarsity Press, 1989), 12.

I wait *for the* LORD, my soul waits,
  and in his word I hope. (Ps. 130:5)

We find the same thing in the New Testament. Waiting is linked to other words and ideas connected to the activity of God:

We wait eagerly *for adoption* as sons. (Rom. 8:23)

. . . waiting *for our blessed hope.* (Titus 2:13)

. . . waiting *for* and hastening *the coming of the day of God.* (2 Pet. 3:12)

Putting this together, we can see that biblical waiting is connected to what we're looking for or where we place our trust. In this way, the gaps of life present an opportunity for faith. Sometimes the translators use "hope" for the same word translated as "wait" in other verses (see Ps. 69:6; Isa. 8:17; Jer. 14:22). That's because waiting and hope are overlapping ideas.

To wait is to look with hope.

Andrew Murray wrote one of the best books on this subject in the 1800s. Remember what I said about "old school"? He divided *waiting on God* into thirty-one devotional chapters, a chapter for each day of a month. It's a goldmine of biblical truth and time-tested counsel. You'll find a lot of Murray quotations in my book, because I think his passion needs to be recovered. Additionally, this classic work shaped my understanding of waiting on God more than any other. Here's a great summary of his main message: "This is the blessedness of waiting upon God, that it takes our eyes and thoughts away from ourselves, even our needs and desires, and occupies us with our God."[3] As I said in the introduction, I'm going to point you toward this vision of waiting: living on what you know to be true about God when you don't know what's true about your life. When practiced correctly, it means embracing the gaps in life as an opportunity to place our hope in God.

Biblical waiting looks to the Lord.

Unfortunately, our waiting doesn't always lead us that direction. We often fill the gaps of life with something else. This struggle with waiting shows us where we place our trust when we're not in control.

Waiting reveals what we hope in. That can be good or bad.

And it's usually hard.

Wasted Waiting

The Bible gives us examples of wasted waiting, and it's connected to times that are challenging. The psalmist made this summary statement:

> They soon forgot his works;
> > they did not wait for his counsel.
> But they had a wanton craving in the wilderness,
> > and put God to the test. (Ps. 106:13–14)

Notice the connection between the failure to wait and misplaced desire.

There are several biblical examples from which we can learn, but let me highlight two of the most famous. Both take place just

---

3. Andrew Murray, *Waiting on God! Daily Messages for a Month* (New York: Revell, 1896), 54–55.

after the exodus. They show us the difficulty with waiting and give us some hints as to why it's so hard.

"Why Did You Bring Us Here?"

The first example is at the shore of the Red Sea. What's remarkable about this moment is not only the lack of faith but how quickly it happened. There's nearly a revolt against Moses's leadership. The people faced a major spiritual crisis.

In Exodus 7–12, the Bible records the miraculous deliverance through the ten plagues. The Israelites witnessed God's awesome power. They experienced his divine protection. God kept his promise. They saw it firsthand. But their confidence didn't last long.

In front of them was an obstacle that appeared to be impossible—the Red Sea. Behind them was a threat that seemed certain to destroy them—the fast-approaching Egyptian army. After Pharaoh's rage-filled change of heart, he pursued the people of God. In the distance they could probably see the dust cloud of a massive army approaching. They were trapped. It didn't look good.

That's when the accusations started flying:

"You're going to get us killed!"
"What were you thinking?"
"We told you this wasn't a good idea."
"This was a mistake. We should go back." (See Ex. 14:11–12)

These statements were unfair, loaded, and foolish. But I'm sure you're familiar with them. They're common when emotions are running high. You can probably think of a time in your life when waiting led you to say things that were rash and spiritually immature. Panic often creates sinful responses. I have a lot of examples, and I'm sure you do too.

This moment in Israel's history became a classic example of a failure to wait.

You may know the rest of the story. God parted the Red Sea, delivering his people and destroying Pharaoh and his army. It became a signature moment of divine deliverance. But before the waters parted, Moses famously rebuked the people: "The LORD will fight for you, and you have only to be silent [or wait]" (Ex. 14:14).

For the purposes of this chapter, I'd like for you to think about those unfair statements hurled at Moses. They were formed in the gap of living between an impassable Red Sea and certain destruction at the hand of Pharaoh. Where do you think those accusations were coming from? In other words, what's the motivation? Try to diagnose what's behind their verbal assaults. What kind of loss of control do you think they felt? We might not be able to sympathize with the pressure that the Israelites were under, but think about what's behind their response. While you are pondering your answers, there's another classic failure to consider.

"We Don't Know What Happened to Him!"

The second major failure takes place at the base of Mount Sinai. It's the tragic story surrounding the golden calf, an infamous moment of idolatry. Exodus 32 recounts that the people pressured Aaron into creating an idol to worship while Moses was on top of the mountain. The people gave up their golden jewelry that had been given to them as they left Egypt. They built the golden calf and worshiped it by saying, "These are your gods, O Israel, who brought you up out of the land of Egypt" (v. 4). It's a bit crazy, considering the deliverance they witnessed a few weeks earlier. But it gets worse. They created a festival and "rose up to play" (v. 6), which is a euphemism for engaging in sexual immorality. The contrast between Moses receiving the Ten Commandments on the mountain while God's people engage in detestable idolatry is stunning. It's an egregious example of rebellion.

But it didn't just happen.

There was a failure to wait.

Exodus 32 is clear: "When the people saw that Moses delayed to come down from the mountain, the people gathered themselves together to Aaron and said to him, 'Up, make us gods who shall go before us. As for this Moses . . . we do not know what has become of him'" (v. 1). God called Moses up the mountain. Forty days transpired, and his absence created a gap, an emotional space that surfaced powerful and problematic emotions. At the Red Sea, they failed to trust in God's deliverance. But at Mount Sinai, they embraced the unfaithfulness of idolatry—"Make us gods." They created alternative gods that gave them a sense of control. They filled the gaps in their life with fake gods.

A failure to wait can lead to spiritual decline and terrible choices.

Once again, I'd like you to diagnose the problem. Can you name the emotions and struggles that the Israelites were facing at the base of Mount Sinai? Put yourself into the text. What would you feel if your leader vanished for forty days with no timeline or communication? What sense of control was lost? What "pushes your buttons" when it comes to waiting? When are you tempted to say, "This is ridiculous!"? And where do you turn when uncertainty, fear, or anxiety becomes overwhelming?

As you consider these two examples from the Old Testament and some self-reflection, notice the power of these gap-filling responses. They're not small issues. This is serious stuff. Waiting pushes our limits. Horrible things are said. Regrettable actions follow.

Sometimes we don't get waiting right because we're not prepared for how hard it is.

When Is Waiting Hard?

One of the ways we waste our waiting is not reckoning with how hard it is and why that's the case. Think back to your diagnosis with the previous two examples from Exodus. Consider some examples of waiting in your own life. Let's see if we can unpack when it's hard so we can understand why.

Uncertainty

Waiting usually involves some level of uncertainty, and that's uncomfortable. It's challenging to move forward when you don't know what's going on or when information is not available. Without data or explanation, problems are hard to prevent or manage. That can feel threatening because information creates solutions. It's important to understand, however, that our desire to possess knowledge is more than a passion for learning. You've probably heard that "knowledge is power." It's true. Knowing what is happening is one of the many ways we try to bring order to our lives.

Previous generations were more familiar with uncertainty. We have faster technologies in our pockets than our grandparents could have ever dreamed. All it takes is a quick internet search, and we can have the answers to most of our questions. Social media gives us a constant update on the lives of our friends. Want to know what's happening around the world? We're only a click or swipe away from instant access to breaking news. All of this creates an unfamiliarity and discomfort with uncertainty.

Waiting for information creates a painful gap. It's hard because understanding what is happening gives us a sense of control.

Uncertainty reveals vulnerability.

Delays

Waiting on the timing of something is also hard. This is probably one of the first examples that people give when talking about waiting. They express audible groans with things like traffic jams, being put on hold, doctor's appointments, airport layovers, or visiting the department of motor vehicles. Our internal clock begins to tick, and we wrestle with why something is taking so long. Add into the mix a slow teller, a demanding customer, or someone trying to cut in line, and it's quite surprising what kind of negative and sinful emotions emerge.

Important and serious moments in life often involve delays, and it isn't easy. Sometimes it's downright scary. I've been a pastor long enough to see the deep tension that develops as people are waiting for a job offer, the sale of a home, college admissions, medical tests, an adoption ruling, or hearing from an estranged family member. These life-altering scenarios usually involve waiting, and it's a battle not to fill the time gap with impatience or fear.

Daily life involves challenging delays.

Disappointment

It's hard to wait when good desires go unfulfilled. There's a unique internal battle when you are waiting for something important, yet you feel the looming clouds of disappointment starting to form. I have in mind a young man or woman who desires the lifelong companionship of marriage or a couple struggling with infertility after years of challenges. There are parents tearfully waiting for their grown children to come back to a relationship with Jesus, and family members who desperately want to see a loved one freed from an addiction because of the havoc it's creating.

This kind of waiting doesn't merely involve information or time. It's connected to dreams and hopes. Often they're honorable desires, and that can make waiting even more challenging. In other words, the fact that it's hard doesn't mean it's wrong.

However, this can quickly devolve. Wrestling with unfulfilled desires or unmet expectations can be deeply painful—even jarring. You might ask, "Why would God make me wait for something that's good?" Betsy Childs Howard writes, "It's much easier to stop hoping than it is to have your dream deferred again and again."[4] How true. For some, this can lead to hopelessness.

Waiting is hard when you've been disappointed.

Pain

It's uncomfortable to wait, and that's especially true when you're in pain. This chapter began with a verse from Psalm 69. I hope you didn't miss the phrase "My eyes grow dim with waiting for my God" (v. 3). David expresses a deep weariness as he cries out to God while being overwhelmed, slandered, rejected, and mocked. In verse 29 he says, "I am afflicted and in pain." The

4. Betsy Childs Howard, *Seasons of Waiting: Walking by Faith When Dreams Are Delayed* (Wheaton, IL: Crossway, 2016), 11.

background isn't entirely clear, but it seems that he's waiting for vindication while being hurt by people. It's hard to wait when you're being attacked.

There are other kinds of pain as well. Many Christians know the challenges related to an illness, a disability, or an ongoing health issue. While medical treatments provide much more relief and healing than in any previous generation, there are still many people waiting for healing. Others are familiar with the slow demise of a loved one. Whether it's the decline with a disease like Alzheimer's or the bedside vigil of hospice care, waiting with a loved one in pain can be heartbreaking. Maybe your pain is related to a relationship conflict, a divorce, a wayward child, or the death of someone close to you.

Waiting for healing—physical and emotional—is hard.

Powerlessness

This is not an exhaustive list, and I'll conclude with the most familiar and applicable category. Waiting is hard when we feel powerless. The gaps of life are really moments with a control vacuum. It might be better to say that waiting is hard *because* we feel powerless.

Therefore, you could easily expand my list into any area where you've lost the kind of control that you want. Information, timing, expectations, and comfort are often able to be managed. When they're not at our disposal, a gap is created, and we have to wait. Can you think of any areas I've not listed? Where do you experience a deep need for control? Consider something that, if missing in your life, creates a significant struggle.

Underneath our disdain for waiting is our longing for control.

Let me be clear on something. That desire isn't fundamentally sinful. Nor is it necessarily wrong if waiting is hard. As we'll see in the coming chapters, gaps in life are part of God's design for the world. They're a common element of our human experience for good reason. Imagine what you'd be like if you didn't have to wait for anything!

We need to wrestle with these questions: When and why is waiting hard?

An Opportunity

Diagnosing when waiting is hard helps us not to waste it. There's an opportunity presented to us that isn't easy, but it's good. And the challenge we experience could be seen as part of the normal Christian life. "The tension you feel as you try to simultaneously hope in heaven while living wholeheartedly in this life isn't necessarily an indicator of sinful discontentment. It may simply be evidence that you are a citizen of heaven living on earth."[5]

The fact that waiting is hard doesn't mean you've already failed.

The simple acknowledgment that it isn't easy, examining why, and then looking to God is the first step of learning how to wait.

Reflection Questions

1. Why do you think this book started with this chapter?

2. Share your diagnoses of the two failures in the Old Testament.

3. Review the list of examples. Which of the five do you resonate with the most? Why?

5. Howard, *Seasons of Waiting*, 107.

4. Why is it helpful to understand when and why waiting is hard?

5. Describe a situation in your life (past or present) where waiting was challenging. What do you think was/is the main reason it was hard?

6. Can you predict the solutions that will be offered later in the book?

2

Frequently

Waiting Is Common

*Be patient, therefore, brothers, until the coming of the
Lord. See how the farmer waits for the precious fruit
of the earth, being patient about it, until it receives the
early and the late rains. You also, be patient. Establish
your hearts, for the coming of the Lord is at hand.*

JAMES 5:7–8

"YOU CAN'T BUY MANNA IN BULK."[1]

This statement made me nearly laugh out loud when I read
it. It's so true. It's a helpful reminder. I'm always stunned at the
bulk quantities at Costco. Who really needs a pack of fifty rolls
of toilet paper, 120 K-Cups, or five pounds of dark roast coffee?
It's one thing if you own a restaurant or manage a small hotel.

---

1. Betsy Childs Howard, *Seasons of Waiting: Walking by Faith When Dreams Are Delayed*
(Wheaton, IL: Crossway, 2016), 88.

However, that's not the norm for most of us. Maybe it's cheaper to buy in bulk. I get that. But I think there's something else that makes large quantities appealing.

Buying in bulk gives us a sense of security. Do you remember the empty shelves in the toilet paper aisles at the start of the COVID pandemic? There's something comforting in reducing any "need gap" that could emerge in our lives.

Manna, however, didn't work like that.

God designed it that way.

For forty years the Israelites wandered in the wilderness. It was more than a wasteland experience. The wilderness became a place of instruction, testing, and waiting. An entire generation was banned from the promised land. Until a new population emerged, they wandered and waited. In the meantime, the Israelites learned to trust God's daily provision.

Manna first appeared in Exodus 16. After the Israelites complained because they didn't have enough food, God provided in a unique way: "Morning by morning they gathered it [manna], each as much as he could eat; but when the sun grew hot, it melted" (Ex. 16:21). If the people attempted to store up food on any day besides the Sabbath, it "bred worms and stank" (16:20). God provided just enough manna for each day. By my calculation, the Israelites went to bed 14,600 times, waiting for God to provide food the next day.

The daily provision of manna created a vital lesson.

It appears in the New Testament in the Lord's Prayer: "Give us this day our daily bread" (Matt. 6:11). The idea is simple and yet profound: God provides what we need on his timeline. He gives daily bread. He provides daily grace.

You can't buy manna in bulk.

How does this relate to waiting? In the last chapter we looked honestly at the fact that waiting is hard. The goal was to help you start to uncover root issues causing you to waste your waiting. I invited you to think about the strong desire for control. I'm trying to help you learn to live on what you know to be true about God when you don't know what's true about your life. It's time to take another step.

This chapter explores how often we have to wait, why that's the case, and how we typically respond in ways that are unhelpful.

Frequent Waiting in Life

Waiting is not only hard; it's normal. It's a common part of the world in which we live. It's a frequent experience of every human being. I know this may seem obvious, but don't dismiss this observation too quickly. It seems to me we tend to forget how normal it is to wait, and it shows up in our surprise and annoyance. Just think with me about how many times you've been shocked when waiting enters your life. I'd like to press on this pattern.

The book of James is about how to find joy in the midst of hardship: "Count it all joy, my brothers, when you meet trials of various kinds, for you know that the testing of your faith produces steadfastness" (James 1:2–3). Patience is a familiar theme throughout the book, and it's specifically commanded in chapter 5: "Be patient, therefore, brothers, until the coming of the Lord" (James 5:7). This is an important exhortation, but it's the illustration following the command that I want you to consider:

> Be patient, therefore, brothers, until the coming of the Lord. *See how the farmer waits for the precious fruit of the earth, being patient about it, until it receives the early and the late rains.*

You also, be patient. Establish your hearts, for the coming of
the Lord is at hand. (James 5:7–8)

Do you see what James is doing? To make his point about the
wisdom and normalcy of spiritual patience, he uses an illustration about a farmer. He makes a point about spiritual endurance
through suffering by arguing that waiting is normal.

Consider the poignancy of this farming illustration. After tilling
the soil and planting the seeds, the farmer must wait. There's a lot
of work for him to do, but there's so much he can't control. He's
powerless to manipulate the weather or cause a seed to germinate.
He works hard, but then he waits. If the farmer isn't patient, he
should find a new profession. James uses this illustration to highlight waiting as something that's spiritually valuable and common.

Waiting is as normal for the Christian as it is for the farmer.

Our earthly lives are filled with countless illustrations of this
truth in other ways. Human beings don't have unlimited capaci-
ties. We're not God. On a practical level, this means we're not
all-powerful, all-knowing, or all-present. Limitations are woven
into the created order. God designed it this way.

Consider a few examples. Human beings need sleep—many of
us need more of it! God designed us such that approximately a
third of our life is spent in a semiconscious, mouth-open, drool-
ing state as we wait for an alarm and the sun to rise. Have you
ever sprained an ankle? You may have heard the RICE recovery
plan: rest, ice, compression, and elevation. For as much as medical
technology has advanced, time and rest are essential to healing. As
I write this chapter, my wife and I are waiting for the birth of our
first two grandchildren. Over the last few months, we've watched

with great delight as our daughters-in-law celebrate baby bumps, observe little movements, and share amazing 3D ultrasounds. It's incredible. But there's no way to speed up a pregnancy. Gestational development takes time. The due dates are set. We're just waiting.

This isn't just true physically. It's also true emotionally. I've written about lament in a book, *Dark Clouds, Deep Mercy: Discovering the Grace of Lament*,[2] to help grieving people learn a language to talk to God when they're in pain. But lament isn't a silver bullet or a quick fix. Recovering from anything traumatic takes time. Frankly, that's what makes grief so frightening. It's a slow process with a lot of uncertainty.

Another area relates to relationship challenges. Whether it's a strained friendship, a wayward child, or a struggling marriage, you probably know the emotional challenge of waiting to see where a relationship is headed or if it's going to improve. People change slowly.

These are just a few examples. I'm sure you can highlight many more. If you think back over your previous week or month, you'll find a lot of moments where you had to wait. You may not have even thought about them. And that's really my point. Waiting is normal because of our limitations. It's a part of the created order, the world in which we live.

The challenge, however, comes when something important, expected, or strongly desired comes into the picture. Suddenly, we're surprised or frustrated that we're having to wait. This reaction is becoming even more common because we're being conditioned to wait less. The speed of information is increasing, and it's decreasing our tolerance. There's a conditioning away from seeing

---

2. Mark Vroegop, *Dark Clouds, Deep Mercy: Discovering the Grace of Lament* (Wheaton, IL: Crossway, 2019).

any delay or uncertainty as normal. Chelsea Wald, in her article "Why Your Brain Hates Slowpokes," identifies that the twentieth century witnessed an increase in communication speed by a factor of ten million and an increase in data transmission speed by a factor of ten billion.[3] That's a staggering increase. Everything is happening a million times faster. Waiting feels less tolerable.

> The fast pace of society has thrown our internal timer out of balance. It creates expectations that can't be rewarded fast enough—or rewarded at all. When things move more slowly than we expect, our internal timer even plays tricks on us, stretching out the wait, summoning anger out of proportion to the delay.[4]

We'll explore several common responses, such as anger, at the end of this chapter. For now, I want you to reflect on how often your life is emotionally affected by waiting. Think back to some major transitions in your life. Whether it was a college acceptance, a dating relationship, a job transfer, a marriage proposal, a pregnancy, or a medical diagnosis, waiting is usually part of the dynamic. Limitations are a part of everyone's story.

Waiting is not just hard; it's common.

That's why the farming illustration in the book of James is so instructive. One way that we can stop wasting our waiting is not to be so surprised when it happens. I've found this to be practically helpful. As I've written this book, it's raised my awareness of the frequency of waiting, and I find myself being less shocked when

---

3. Chelsea Wild, "Why Your Brain Hates Slowpokes," *Nautilus*, March 2, 2015, accessed January 21, 2023, https://nautil.us/.
4. Wild, "Why Your Brain Hates Slowpokes."

it happens. It's a simple shift, and I'm a bit embarrassed about the prideful assumptions and desire for control that were underneath my surprise when it happened in the past.

Embracing that life is filled with opportunities to wait is liberating.

Frequent Waiting in the Bible

Waiting is not only common in life; it's also frequently found in the Bible. Manna is just one example.

If you think about your favorite Bible characters, you'll find some moments when they lived in an uncomfortable gap. Peter Scazzero highlights a few notable examples:

> Abraham waited almost twenty-five years for God to follow through on his promise of the birth of Isaac. Joseph waited somewhere between thirteen and twenty-two years to see his family again after being betrayed by his brothers. Moses waited forty years in the desert for God to resurrect a purpose for his life. Hannah waited years for an answer to her prayers for a child. Job waited years, not months, for God to reveal himself, redeem his losses, and take him into a new beginning. John the Baptist and Jesus waited almost thirty years before the Father's time for their ministries came to fulfillment.[5]

There are many more examples throughout the pages of Scripture. Frankly it's hard to find a spiritual leader who didn't face seasons

5. Peter Scazzero, *The Emotionally Healthy Leader: How Transforming Your Inner Life Will Deeply Transform Your Church, Team, and the World* (Grand Rapids, MI: Zondervan, 2015), 282–83.

of agonizing waiting. The reason might be factually obvious, but it's important to embrace this emotionally: "waiting for God is one of the central experiences of the Christian life."[6]

It's no wonder that this theme made its way into the songs God's people sang. A quick search reveals fourteen different psalms that celebrate waiting. Here are a few examples:

> To you, O Lord, I lift up my soul.
>> O my God, in you I trust;
>> let me not be put to shame;
>> let not my enemies exult over me.
> Indeed, none who wait for you shall be put to shame.
>> (Ps. 25:1–3)

> I believe that I shall look upon the goodness of the Lord
>> in the land of the living!
> Wait for the Lord;
>> be strong, and let your heart take courage;
>> wait for the Lord! (Ps. 27:13–14)

> I waited patiently for the Lord;
>> he inclined to me and heard my cry. (Ps. 40:1)

More than any other book in the Bible, Psalms records the heart language of God's people. In their struggle and through their faith, they kept seeking God's help. It's no wonder that waiting appears often, because every believer has seasons of waiting.

---

6. Scazzero, *Emotionally Healthy Leader*, 282.

Waiting is also found in the writings of the Old Testament prophets as God's people longed for their promised deliverance:

I will wait for the LORD, who is hiding his face from the house of Jacob, and I will hope in him. (Isa. 8:17)

O LORD, be gracious to us; we wait for you.
    Be our arm every morning,
    our salvation in the time of trouble. (Isa. 33:2)

So you, by the help of your God, return,
    hold fast to love and justice,
    and wait continually for your God. (Hos. 12:6)

But as for me, I will look to the LORD;
    I will wait for the God of my salvation;
    my God will hear me. (Mic. 7:7)

During seasons of uncertainty or suffering, God's people struggled to persevere. Learning to wait on God was an act of faith as they tried to make sense of painful circumstances. Desperation fueled their spiritual longing. Waiting on God was both how they survived and how they lived with hope.

The New Testament features this theme as well. Even after the dawn of redemption, we're still waiting. Both Paul and Peter use it as a central calling of every Christian:

For we know that the whole creation has been groaning together in the pains of childbirth until now. And not only the creation, but we ourselves, who have the firstfruits of the Spirit, groan inwardly as we wait eagerly for adoption as sons, the redemption of our bodies. For in this hope we were saved. Now hope that is seen is not hope. For who hopes for what he sees? But if we hope for what we do not see, we wait for it with patience. (Rom. 8:22–25)

Since all these things are thus to be dissolved, what sort of people ought you to be in lives of holiness and godliness, waiting for and hastening the coming of the day of God. (2 Pet. 3:11–12)

Waiting isn't a supplemental experience of the Christian life. It's central. Following Jesus involves a life of waiting.

Beyond the frequency of the use of the word *waiting*, it's also part of the gospel. The plan of redemption involved both the cross and the empty tomb. Jesus died, and he rose again from the dead. It's easy to miss the fact that there was a gap between Good Friday and Resurrection Sunday. Have you ever considered that God could have immediately raised Jesus from the dead after he cried, "It is finished" (John 19:30)? Instead, a time of waiting—days of grief, confusion, and fear—was built into the divine plan.

The more I've studied waiting in the Bible, the more I'm stunned. It's all over the scriptures. It's a key part of most spiritual leaders' story. It's a central part of what it means to be a follower of Jesus.

But it's easy to forget. We get sucked into the speed vortex of our culture. Our desires morph into deep-seated entitlement. We begin to live like everyone else—including fellow Christians—with a relentless pursuit to avoid any encounter with our limitations. Even though waiting is common in the created world, and even though it's a major theme in the Bible, we don't see it that way.

We're shocked and bothered when we must wait.

God designed waiting in the world and in redemption so that he's central, not you or me. The frequency of waiting confronts our desire for control. We'll learn more about this and what to do about it in the chapters that follow.

For now, consider this: *waiting is what you do when you can't do what you want to do.*

Read that again. Slowly, maybe even out loud. It's really important.

Frequent Waiting Errors

The goal of this chapter is to help you understand that waiting is a part of the world in which we live and a frequent theme in the Bible. It's God's design to regularly remind us that we are not divine. We have major limitations for which we need God's help. This is not an accident.

God intends for us to wait on him.

Sadly, I've often learned this lesson the hard way. My typical path is to be surprised at the opportunity to wait. When my desire for control gets the best of me, I frequently turn to three unhelpful and sinful responses: anger, anxiety, and apathy.

Anger

I'm sure you're not shocked to see anger listed as a sinful reaction. It's probably the most common response. We even have a specific cultural name for this as it relates to driving: road rage.

Our last teenager completed driver's training a few years ago. Despite having a bright yellow magnet on our vehicle that said, "Student Driver: Please Be Patient," it was amazing how angry people became when she drove the speed limit or made a slow start at a green light or a cautious righthand turn on red. It didn't take much to create obvious anger in other drivers.

Road rage, however, is merely one example. There are many more because waiting and anger frequently go together. Sometimes it looks like an obvious blowup with hurtful words or rash actions. At other times, it lingers as a low simmer. Maybe you relate through a longstanding disappointment or an unfulfilled dream that creates a baseline of frustration. It feels like you are one unmet expectation away from losing it.

Sinful anger is simply our attempt to take control.

When it comes to waiting, it's tempting to fill the gap of vulnerability with anger. In actuality, anger is just a way for us to force change. Rather than living on what we know to be true about God, we choose to live on what we're going to do—right now! Regardless of the consequences.

Anxiety

If anger is about external action, anxiety is about internal thinking or processing. Anxiety and worry, like anger, are sometimes appropriate. There are things in life that we should be concerned and even worried about. Anyone who cares for another person needs to be mindful of what could happen. Safety precautions are wise.

But the kind of anxiety I have in mind is the constant thinking of potential problems or the persistent ruminating on what could be done to solve an issue. I'm talking about the kind of internal narrative that reacts to fears, insecurities, unfulfilled dreams, and past hurts. It's another way that we respond to the gaps in life and our lack of control. Rather than blowing up, we turn inward with a mental and emotional churning that can be exhausting and debilitating.

Rather than learning to wait on God, we try to think our way out of our limitations.

Apathy

Anger demands action. Anxiety wants to think. Apathy stops caring. It's the person who has responded to disappointment, delays, and unfulfilled dreams with the self-protecting posture of "I just don't care anymore." They've grown weary of hoping, only to be disappointed—again.

Have you heard of the work problem called "quiet quitting"? I started reading more about it over the last few years. It describes employees who show up to work, but they do the bare minimum. They're deeply unmotivated. They're not flourishing. They've stopped caring about their work. They've quit, but they're still at work.

I suspect that there are a fair number of Christians doing the same thing. They still come to church. They still sing. But they've quit hoping as they are waiting. In an effort toward self-protection, they stop hoping in anything, including God. It might seem like they're not waiting anymore because they've given up. Rather than embracing a God-centered hope, they've resigned themselves to no longer wait by quitting on it.

Apathy is just another defense mechanism to control our disappointment.

Do you resonate with these? We often waste our waiting with anger, anxiety, and apathy. Understanding the frequency of waiting and our typical sinful responses can be the first step in change and a path to peace. The Lord promises to help us fight against these wrong responses. We'll learn more about how to do this in the next two chapters. The first step is simply recognizing how common they really are.

To live as a human being in the world means we will have limitations. We can't control everything. Waiting is common. To be a Christian means there's spiritual value in seasons of waiting. It's central to our walk of faith.

God designed waiting to be a frequent part of our lives.

You can't buy manna in bulk.

Reflection Questions

1. Why is it helpful to consider the frequency of waiting in daily living and in the Christian life?

2. Where do you experience the most tension with the loss of control?

3. List some reasons why waiting is good for your maturity and faith.

4. Which of the three responses (anger, anxiety, and apathy) do you struggle with the most? Why do you think that's the case?

5. Write a sentence or two reflecting on the internal narrative (What do I want?) when you give in to that unhelpful response.

6. Before we move into solutions, take some time to write a brief prayer expressing what you are learning.

3

Thoughtfully

Waiting Is Biblical

Lead me in your truth and teach me,
for you are the God of my salvation;
for you I wait all the day long.

PSALM 25:5

"GOD IS GOING TO HELP YOU. He has to."

My wife and I were sitting in our sunroom early in the morning for our daily check-in. This cherished start to our day over a cup of coffee was simply a way to get a pulse on each other. However, that morning my heart was unusually heavy. I was spiritually and emotionally exhausted from so much waiting. I wasn't just tired and in need of rest. I wasn't just weary and in need of encouragement.

Sitting in the sunroom, I shared a brewing sense of hopelessness. I felt disoriented. With tears in my eyes, I said, "I'm really discouraged, even hopeless. I'm not sure how to do this, Sarah."

Waiting had taken a costly toll.

After listening quietly and empathetically, my wife lovingly reminded me about several biblical truths that I believed. She articulated what I knew but had become distorted with my long season of waiting. Then she summarized her counsel with a poignant and spontaneous encouragement: "God's going to help you. He has to."

Her words, certainty, and faith, anchored in the promises of God, buoyed my soul. Sarah exhorted me regarding God's assurance to help me. It's not that I could make him do exactly what I wanted. Rather, it was a calling to live by divine promise. Charles Spurgeon captures this when he writes:

> We are sure that the Lord will continue his blessings to his people. He does not give and take. What he has granted us is the token of much more. That which we have not yet received is as sure as that which has already come. Therefore, let us wait before the Lord and be still. . . . Many things are questionable, but of the Lord we sing "for his mercies shall endure, every faithful, ever sure."[1]

It wasn't a quick fix. The challenges were still very real. However, I needed a simple reminder to focus on what was true about God. The sunroom conversation started to burn away the fog of despair, reorienting my thinking and reconnecting my heart to biblical truth. It helped me take a step of faith. If God said that

---

1. Charles Spurgeon, *The Promises of God: A New Edition of the Classic Devotional Based on the English Standard Version*, ed. Tim Chester (Wheaton, IL: Crossway, 2019), "July 27" entry.

he "acts for those who wait for him" (Isa. 64:4), then I could keep waiting by focusing on what I knew to be true about him. I could take God at his word—again and again.

That simple but powerful statement was the beginning of a new journey, a purposeful commitment to set my mind on who God is and what he promised. Instead of focusing on what I didn't know, I began to intentionally rehearse what I knew was true about God. This didn't make all the challenges or anxiety vanish. The gaps of life remained with more difficulties to come. But it provided an important lesson, one that I'm still trying to learn.

Waiting requires living by what I know to be true about God when I don't know what's true about my life.

Waiting Thoughtfully

The previous sentence should sound familiar. It's the theme of this book, and this chapter explores the first half of that life-giving statement: " . . . living by what I know to be true about God." In the previous chapters, we learned about the struggle with waiting, observing that it's hard and common. But at a deeper level, waiting reveals what we believe about ourselves and about God. It challenges our dreams, expectations, and abilities. Waiting is a frequent and often painful reminder that we're not in control.

God is.

The more I've studied and practiced waiting on God, the more convinced I am that waiting tests what you believe. It requires thinking carefully and theologically. It's an opportunity to use uncertainty as the means of spiritual growth and intimacy with your Savior. Sadly, many of us waste these seasons because we're not thinking this way about our waiting. We're just reacting, emoting, and (usually) sinning.

In this chapter, we'll look more closely at how the Bible defines waiting, sometimes using different words for the same idea. We'll also learn a practical strategy to put into practice. In other words, I hope to show you how to think biblically about waiting and how to do it.

Sarah was right.

God is going to help you. He has to.

Biblical Waiting

At this point you shouldn't be surprised that waiting is biblical, as we've seen through several passages already. Hopefully you are starting to see not only how this theme is woven into the fabric of our humanity, but also how it's a vital part of discipleship.

To be a Christian requires waiting.

What exactly does the Bible mean when it talks about waiting? That's an important question to answer. And it's not as simple as a singular word. In fact, there are different Hebrew and Greek words used in the Bible.

Old Testament Waiting

The most common word for waiting in the Old Testament is *qavah*. It's used forty-seven times from Genesis to Malachi, and the meaning is "to look with eager expectation."[2] In chapter 1, I highlighted this basic definition as a starting point, but there's more to consider. *Qavah* is a word filled with action and purpose.

2. John E. Hartley, "1994 קָוָה," in *Theological Wordbook of the Old Testament*, ed. R. Laird Harris, Gleason L. Archer Jr., and Bruce K. Waltke (Chicago: Moody, 1999), 791.

It has the idea of looking forward to something or the arrival of someone. But it's also a word with tension. One Hebrew lexicon connects the origins of the word to the twisting or stretching of a cord.[3] You could think of *qavah* as looking with hope in the tension of life. The books of Psalms and Isaiah are filled with bold and faith-filled passages that use this word:

> I believe that I shall look upon the goodness of the LORD
>   in the land of the living!
> *Wait* for the LORD;
>   be strong, and let your heart take courage;
>   *wait* for the LORD! (Ps. 27:13–14)

> I *waited* patiently for the LORD;
>   he inclined to me and heard my cry. (Ps. 40:1)

> O LORD, be gracious to us; we *wait* for you.
>   Be our arm every morning,
>   our salvation in the time of trouble. (Isa. 33:2)

> But they who *wait* for the LORD shall renew their strength;
>   they shall mount up with wings like eagles;
> they shall run and not be weary;
>   they shall walk and not faint. (Isa. 40:31)

These passages help us to see that biblical waiting is active and intentional, especially when life gets twisted and complicated.

---

3. Francis Brown, Samuel Rolles Driver, and Charles Augustus Briggs, *Enhanced Brown-Driver-Briggs Hebrew and English Lexicon* (Oxford, UK: Clarendon Press, 1977), 875.

I don't know about you, but that's not how I've typically thought about waiting. It feels more like empty space. It seems to be entirely passive, something happening to me. *Qavah* helps us to see waiting as purposeful, even productive. But we must start by thinking biblically.

We fill the tension-filled gaps of life with looking to God.

The second most common word is *yahal*. It's used forty-two times in the Old Testament, and the nuance is more directly tied to confidence or hope.[4] In fact, the translators of the Septuagint, the Greek translation of the Hebrew Old Testament, often used the Greek word *hope* for this Hebrew word.

> Be strong, and let your heart take courage,
> all you who *wait* for the LORD! (Ps. 31:24)

> But for you, O LORD, do I *wait*;
> it is you, O Lord my God, who will answer. (Ps. 38:15)

To *wait* and *hope* are interchangeable in the Bible. That's another unique nuance. Most of my waiting doesn't naturally involve a lot of hope. Rather, my typical response is annoyance at best and anger at worst. You too? Understanding the biblical connection between *wait* and *hope* invites us to shift our focus from what's not true about our lives to what is true about God. In other words, waiting biblically is seeing seasons of delay as opportunities to hope in God.

The final word is *hakah*. It's more connected to spiritual patience than the other Hebrew words. Often it is related to trusting in

---

4. Paul R. Gilchrist, "859 יָחַל," in *Theological Wordbook of the Old Testament*, 373–74.

the promises of God, especially through painful circumstances
or challenges:

> Our soul *waits* for the LORD;
>> he is our help and our shield. (Ps. 33:20)

> I will *wait* for the LORD, who is hiding his face from the house
> of Jacob, and I will hope in him. (Isa. 8:17)

> From of old no one has heard
>> or perceived by the ear,
> no eye has seen a God besides you,
>> who acts for those who *wait* for him. (Isa. 64:4)

Waiting is the spiritual posture of endurance. Often this is
because pain or suffering is mingled into the uncertainty. We'll
explore what it means to wait patiently in the next chapter. But
here, it's important to understand that waiting on God is how we
respond to difficult delays.

Putting this together, it's clear that biblical waiting is active and
intentional when life is filled with tension. It's connected to hope
and trust. A prime example of this is Psalm 130:5. The psalmist
uses the same Hebrew word (*qavah*) three times in verse 5, but
our translations correctly use different English words (*wait, hope*).
"I wait for the LORD, my soul waits, and in his word I hope"
(Ps. 130:5). This is important.

It's not just that waiting and hope work together. They're the
same thing! In other words, you don't just wait with hope or wait
with faith. From a biblical perspective, to wait is to hope. To wait

is to trust. To wait is to have faith. This requires courage. Andrew Murray affirms this when he writes:

> One of the chief needs in our waiting upon God, one of the deepest secrets of its blessedness and blessing, is a quiet, confident persuasion that it is not in vain; courage to believe that God will hear and help.[5]

To wait on God is to believe that he will help you.

New Testament Waiting

The meaning is similar in the New Testament. There's nothing passive about waiting on God. In fact, there are two foundational meanings: to receive and to watch. Both imply a particular kind of activity.

To receive or accept (*dechomai*) is the most common way that the New Testament talks about waiting. The difference is the prepositions *from*, *to*, or *toward*. The main point is that the person waiting has a need outside of him- or herself. The gap creates the need to receive something or to welcome it.[6] It's a posture of open hands, a spiritual opportunity to receive from God. There are a number of verses where this is evident, but consider these two:

> Keep yourselves in the love of God, *waiting* for the mercy of our Lord Jesus Christ that leads to eternal life. (Jude 21)

5. Andrew Murray, *Waiting on God! Daily Messages for a Month* (New York: Revell, 1896), 45–46.
6. Aaron C. Fenlason, "Hope," in *Lexham Theological Wordbook*, ed. Douglas Mangum et al., Lexham Bible Reference Series (Bellingham, WA: Lexham Press, 2014).

Through the Spirit, by faith, we ourselves eagerly *wait* for the hope of righteousness. (Gal. 5:5)

As you can see, waiting is directly tied to what is anticipated. In Jude 21, it's mercy. In Galatians 5, it's the hope of righteousness. These verses shape our understanding of waiting as something inherently spiritual. At least, it could be that way if we connect waiting to what God provides.

The other word in the New Testament, *prosdokao*, relates to watching.[7] However, it's not a passive word either. The idea is an intentional effort to look for something. Don't think of this word as being like watching a baseball game. It's more like a guard scanning the horizon. There's a sense of anticipation implied in the word, and we see this clearly in 2 Peter 3:

Since all these things are thus to be dissolved, what sort of people ought you to be in lives of holiness and godliness, waiting for and hastening the coming of the day of God. . . . But according to his promise we are waiting for new heavens and a new earth in which righteousness dwells. (vv. 11–13)

Peter is encouraging suffering Christians to direct their attention and be alert to the future. He points them to judgment day ("the coming day of God") and the new heavens and new earth. The idea is to live with a posture of spiritual watchfulness. Waiting in this context isn't something that happens to you; it's an intentional way of life as a Christian.

7. James Strong, *A Concise Dictionary of the Words in the Greek Testament and The Hebrew Bible* (Bellingham, WA: Logos Bible Software, 2009), 61.

From both the Old and New Testaments, we get a clear picture of biblical waiting. Isn't it different from how we normally think about it? The definitions and assumptions in the words we use aren't the same. In fact, our English dictionaries define *waiting* as "a pause, interval, or delay."[8] While some definitions get closer to the biblical concept (e.g., "to stay in a place of expectation"),[9] others are more familiar to our common experience (e.g., "to remain in a state of temporary inactivity").[10] The difference between the biblical ideal and how we typically understand waiting is one of the reasons I've written this book. As we've learned in previous chapters, we don't need to waste the gap moments. Instead, we can embrace them as a spiritual opportunity if we allow the Bible to shape our thinking.

Not wasting our waiting requires approaching it thoughtfully.

That's what my wife was doing in the sunroom. She reminded me of what I knew was true. I needed a spiritual reorientation. What's more, she redirected my attention and what I was thinking about. I needed a different focus. It helped. This wasn't the only time I had to recalibrate my perspective. But the first step was to think differently about my waiting. Maxie Dunnam, the former president of Asbury Seminary, quoted a testimony of a ministry colleague who illustrates this perspective:

> I'm in the middle of that decision right now, and I'm not get-
> ting any direction, but I'm feeling close to the Lord because I'm
> struggling. I'm dependent. I feel in resonance with the Spirit;

8. *Dictionary.com*, s.v. "waiting," accessed March 24, 2023, https://www.dictionary.com/.
9. *Merriam-Webster*, s.v. "waiting," accessed March 24, 2023, https://www.merriam-webster.com/.
10. *Merriam-Webster*, s.v. "waiting."

while I don't have an answer, I'm where God wants me to be because I'm focused on him.[11]

Looking to God with hopeful watching and faith-filled receiving is what it means to wait.

A Strategy for Biblical Waiting

How do we make this practical? I'm sure you're reading this book because you'd like to move from anxiety to faith-filled, hopeful waiting. Now that we understand how the Bible defines waiting, let me give you a fourfold strategy from Psalm 25.

First, imagine an uncomfortable or stressful situation where you're not in control. Try to recollect a recent scenario to make it more vivid and personal. It's probably not hard to find a few examples. Ask yourself what dynamics are in play, what thoughts flood your mind, what fears are surfacing, and what you want. Just to be clear, I'm not assuming that every answer to the previous questions is bad or sinful. Often the things we desire are good, and we might have an understandable reason to be concerned. Our struggle with waiting isn't implicitly sinful. It can be, but it depends on what we do next. In the previous chapter, I identified three unhelpful responses: anger, anxiety, and apathy. What's the solution?

Focus. Adore. Seek. Trust.

I'm not a huge fan of acronyms. Sometimes they seem forced. But I'm going to break my own rule, because when waiting

---

11. Maxie Dunnam, "A Heart Close to God," in *Deepening Your Ministry through Prayer and Personal Growth: 30 Strategies to Transform Your Ministry*, ed. Marshall Shelley (Nashville, TN: Moorings, 1996), 41.

becomes disorienting, you need a memorable path out of the fog. When your thinking is off and the internal tension is rising, I hope you'll remember to wait FAST: focus, adore, seek, and trust.

This process is a distillation of four principles from Psalm 25.

Focus

The first step is changing our focus. Uncertainty or scenarios where we're not in control tend to take over our thoughts and emotions. It sounds like this:

"What's going on? Why is this taking so long?"

"I haven't heard anything yet. It must mean . . . "

"I'm getting nervous. I need to start taking some steps."

"What have I done wrong that I can't get an answer?"

"Is God really listening to me?"

When you're in this frame of mind, it's easy to be singularly focused on what you don't know or what you don't have. It can occupy a lot of energy.

The first step is recognizing this pattern and turning it into a spiritual opportunity. Instead of living with a "gap-centered" mindset, you can choose to live with a God-centered perspective. In this way, the loss of control becomes a means of spiritual growth. But it starts with changing your focus.

We see this intentional shift in Psalm 25:1–3. The context of the psalm appears to be some kind of conflict with people. David describes himself as lonely, afflicted, troubled, and distressed (vv. 16–17). So it must have been intense. But the psalm begins with hopeful purpose:

> To you, O LORD, I lift up my soul.
> O my God, in you I trust;
> > let me not be put to shame;
> > let not my enemies exult over me.
> Indeed, none who wait for you shall be put to shame. (vv. 1–3a)

Rather than wasting his waiting by being angry or anxious, David directs his focus to the Lord. Remember the meaning of the biblical words for *waiting*? They invite us to see it as receiving from the Lord or to look to him.

This first step may be the hardest since the emotional power of the "gap moment" is strong. But if we can intentionally make this shift, there's a lot of hope. Andrew Murray compares it to moving into the sunshine:

> Come, and however feeble you feel, just wait in His presence. As a feeble, sickly invalid is brought out into the sunshine to let its warmth go through him, come with all that is dark and cold in you into the sunshine of God's holy, omnipotent love, and sit and wait there, with the one thought: Here I am, in the sunshine of His love. As the sun does its work in the weak one who seeks its rays, God will do His work in you.[12]

12. Murray, *Waiting on God!*, 48.

Change your focus. Don't live by what you don't know about your life. Embrace this truth instead: "None who wait for you shall be put to shame" (Ps. 25:3).

Adore

The second step is to worshipfully rehearse what you know to be true about God. Waiting chooses to focus on what I know about the Lord instead of panicking in uncertainty. This step intentionally fills the gaps of life with the glory of God as we think about him.

Reframe your internal question from "What's missing?" to "What's true about God?"

In Psalm 25:5 we see this worshipful posture: "For you are the God of my salvation; for you I wait all the day long." This is more than a statement of facts. David links waiting and worship. He's filling the gaps of life with adoration.

After my sunroom conversation with my wife, I put this into practice by memorizing Psalm 27:1: "The LORD is my light and my salvation; whom shall I fear? The LORD is the stronghold of my life; of whom shall I be afraid?" Rather than focusing on the words "fear" and "afraid," I emphasized who the Lord is. Sometimes I'd even say the word "is" with greater emphasis to make the point stronger in my soul: "The LORD IS my light. . . . The LORD IS the stronghold of my life." Since glory is connected to weightiness, I imagined the truth of God taking up all the space in my gap moment.

Filling my waiting with who God is proved to be transforming.

Psalms 25 and 27, however, are just the start. I found it helpful to meditate on and rehearse other verses. In the appendix you'll find two lists of verses: "The Lord Is . . . " and "Lord, You Are . . . " Use these lists as a way to fill up your waiting with worship.

Biblical waiting intentionally fills the gaps of life with adoration.

Seek

The third step involves inviting and requesting God's help. It's another step in making waiting something active. It's easy to make the mistake of thinking that waiting means we are doing nothing. However, biblical waiting means that I'm seeking God's help in a new and even desperate way.

We see numerous purposeful requests for divine deliverance in Psalm 25. Here are just a few:

Turn to me and be gracious to me. (v. 16)

Bring me out of my distresses. (v. 17)

Consider my affliction and my trouble. (v. 18)

Guard my soul. (v. 20)

Deliver me! (v. 20)

That's a lot of requests! And that's what we do when we wait. We're not in control, so we talk to the one who is. We don't know, so we seek the one who does. Eugene Peterson says this:

Hoping does not mean doing nothing. It is not fatalistic resignation. It means going about our assigned tasks, confident that God will provide the meaning and the conclusions. It is not compelled to work away at keeping up appearances with a bogus spirituality. It is the opposite of desperate and panicky manipulations, of scurrying and worrying.[13]

Don't make the mistake of thinking that waiting means you are doing nothing. Usually it just means that you're not doing what you want to do.

Biblical waiting is active; it seeks the Lord.

Trust

The final step is embracing by faith the contentment and spiritual rest that come from knowing God can be trusted. This is where focusing, adoring, and seeking lead us. Waiting involves affirming what we know and learning to live on it. That doesn't mean all our questions will be answered. Nor does it mean the waiting will be over soon.

At the end of Psalm 25 it's clear that David is still in the middle of uncertainty. There's remaining fear in the air. But he chooses to wait on God.

Consider how many are my foes,
and with what violent hatred they hate me.
Oh, guard my soul, and deliver me!
Let me not be put to shame, for I take refuge in you.
May integrity and uprightness preserve me,
for I wait for you.

13. Eugene H. Peterson, *A Long Obedience in the Same Direction: Discipleship in an Instant Society*, commemorative ed. (Downers Grove, IL: InterVarsity Press, 2019), 138.

Redeem Israel, O God,
  out of all his troubles. (vv. 19–22)

This hopeful, trusting posture is expressed in Psalm 27 as well:

I believe that I shall look upon the goodness of the LORD
  in the land of the living!
Wait for the LORD;
  be strong, and let your heart take courage;
  wait for the LORD!" (vv. 13–14)

Waiting embraces God as a refuge while the answers are not clear and may never be.

What's your strategy when you have to wait? Instead of allowing strong emotions to overtake you, use FAST as a framework to turn waiting into a spiritual opportunity. I've seen firsthand the practical benefits of engaging my mind and heart in this way. When a gap moment emerges, and I feel the rising tide of worry, it's been helpful to shift FAST—to focus, adore, seek, and trust. I'm learning to battle anxiety and frustration with this biblical strategy. The next time you face uncertainty, delays, or a sense of powerlessness, I hope you'll start to embrace waiting by reminding yourself what you know to be true about God when you don't know what's true about your life.

Waiting requires living thoughtfully. While we acknowledge our uncertainty and the challenges of the moment, we can reorient our thinking. In so doing, we can maximize our waiting instead of wasting it. Andrew Murray offers this helpful summary:

You are not going to wait on yourself to see what you feel and what changes come to you. You are going to wait on God, to know *first*, what He is, and then, after that, what He will do.[14]

In other words, God is going to help you. He has to!

Reflection Questions

1. Describe a time when waiting caused great despair in your life.

2. How is biblical waiting fundamentally different from how we normally think about it?

3. What are some barriers in your thinking that stand in the way of biblical waiting?

4. Which of the four steps (FAST) are most challenging for you? Why is that the case?

5. Review the "The Lord Is . . . " and "Lord, You Are . . . " lists in the appendix. Which verses are most meaningful to you and why?

6. How might the principles of this chapter be applied to a waiting situation now or in the future?

---

14. Murray, *Waiting on God!*, 47–48.

4

Patiently

Waiting Is Slow

I waited patiently for the LORD;
he inclined to me and heard my cry.

PSALM 40:1

I DON'T THINK COUNSELORS are supposed to laugh at their
counselee's answers. But mine did. And I quickly joined him
because I suddenly realized how ridiculous I sounded.

Plus it felt good to laugh at myself, especially in a counseling
session.

We were processing some personal hurts and disappointments
that weren't going to be resolved quickly. I was unpacking some
frustrations with myself and the circumstances in my life. As my
counselor sought to understand the root cause of my struggles,
he asked a simple but insightful question: "Mark, tell me about
your expectations." The mere question was jarring. At the time,
I didn't know why. Probably a sign that it was a good question!

Instinctively, I responded, "Oh, I don't have expectations."

That's when he couldn't hold back the chuckle. Then my wife joined in. "What?" I said defensively. "I'm serious. I don't have any expectations."

"Mark," my counselor said with a smile, "everyone has expectations."

That's when we all started laughing—hard. You might think it's a bit strange, but it was funny because I was absolutely convinced that I was living expectation free. Not only was that not true, but it was a major problem. Why?

Because blindness to my expectations created a lot of additional stress, especially with anything related to waiting.

I was unknowingly making difficult things harder. On top of challenging situations, I was adding to my disappointment. Over time I began to see the connection between my impatience and my expectations. Here's what I learned.

Waiting requires patience beyond my expectations.

So far in our journey, we've learned that waiting is not only hard and common, but it's also a major theme in the Bible. In the last chapter I gave you a strategy to employ: focus, adore, seek, and trust (FAST). Hopefully from this strategy you can see that waiting doesn't have to be a waste. You can fill the gap moments of life with spiritual purpose by shifting your perspective from "Why is God allowing this to happen?" to "Who is God?"

In this chapter, we're going to explore how to move from "This isn't what I expected" to "I'm waiting patiently."

Starting at the End of Psalm 40

Psalm 40 may be one of the most familiar passages in the Bible on waiting. Some of us heard it for the first time through a song by

U2 in the eighties. I can still hear the tune and the crowd singing along: "I will sing, sing a new song." I've often heard Psalm 40 quoted at a funeral because of its hopeful posture. When I've visited someone in the hospital, this is a text that I'll read at the bedside because it's a source of deep comfort. Psalm 40 is loaded with encouragement.

Normally we'd follow the flow of the argument in the order of the verses. But to understand this psalm and how it helps us with waiting, we need to start at the end. The last verse says, "You are my help and my deliverer; do not delay, O my God" (Ps. 40:17b). The psalm ends with a hopeful urgency. It embraces who God is (take note!) while pleading for help. Keep this in mind because it frames the rest of the psalm.

Psalm 40 shows us a strategy for patient waiting.

We don't know the circumstances pertaining to why this psalm was written, but we get a few clues. A quick survey reveals David expressing concern for overwhelming problems, his personal failures, and a deeply discouraged heart (v. 12). He's being attacked, and people are delighting in his pain (v. 14). Some desire to gloat over his misery (v. 15). David describes himself as "poor and needy" (v. 17). Whatever the background is, it's clear that there's a desperate need for God's help.

David is waiting for deliverance.

And what he expresses in this psalm helps us understand how to wait patiently.

Redefining Patience

Let's start by changing how we think about the word *patience*. The psalm begins by looking backward. The first verse is probably the most well-known of the entire psalm: "I waited patiently for the LORD" (Ps. 40:1). But you probably don't realize that there's something missing.

It's the word *patiently*.

Now, you might be a bit confused because you just read it. That's true. The major English translations include the word *patiently* in the first verse. But if you were to look in the original Hebrew, you won't find it. There's no word for "patiently" in verse 1. A Hebrew word for *patiently* is available and could have been included. David just didn't use it.

Instead, he merely repeated the word *qavah* ("wait") twice. This led Eugene Peterson to translate Psalm 40:1 this way: "I waited and waited and waited for GOD" (MSG). While there's nothing incorrect about adding the word *patience* to capture the meaning, does "I waited and waited and waited" land on you differently? It does for me. And I've found it helpful. Here's why. It shows me that patience starts by simply waiting more than what I've wanted or expected.

Waiting patiently embraces the uncomfortable addition of more time.

At first that might sound too simplistic. But I don't think it is. I've often thought of patience as requiring a completely different mindset about an experience. That could be true. However, what if *patience* simply means to not quit or give in? What if it means to keep doing what's right? It seems that we could say that patience is more about not doing something different and unhelpful, like reacting or emotionally responding.

The meaning of *patience* in the New Testament confirms this. The most common Greek word (*makrothumia*) refers to "a state of emotional calm in the face of provocation or misfortune and without complaint or irritation."[1] Take note that the definition emphasizes what is present (emotional calm) and what is absent (complaint or irritation). In other words, patience isn't just about what you do, but it's also about what you choose not to do. Louw and Nida, in their Greek-English lexicon, identify the way other languages express this: "In a number of languages 'patience' is expressed idiomatically, for example: 'to remain seated in one's heart' or 'to keep one's heart from jumping' or 'to have a waiting heart.'"[2]

It helps me to think about waiting patiently as simply staying put or not jumping. That's a practical application I need. It changes how I think about what success looks like.

We can also see this if we look back to how the word *patience* was used five hundred years ago. If you are familiar with the King James Bible (1611), the old English word for patience was *longsuffering*. I like this word because it captures my experience in hardship, and it gives me a more tangible goal. Longsuffering simply means to suffer longer. But ask yourself, "Longer than what?" Longer than we expect.

One way Psalm 40 helps us is to reset our understanding of patience. It still includes the right attitude and perspective: a humble dependency. But understanding how my expectations affect my perspective on waiting has been helpful. Patience is formed by letting go of what I thought was going to be true about my life.

I waited and waited and waited for the Lord.

1. Johannes P. Louw and Eugene Albert Nida, *Greek-English Lexicon of the New Testament: Based on Semantic Domains* (New York: United Bible Societies, 1996), 306.
2. Louw and Nida, *Greek-English Lexicon of the New Testament*, 306.

As you think about learning to wait on God, how might your expectations make it more challenging? I'm certainly not the only one with underlying, unspoken expectations. We'll explore this further at the end of the chapter. But for now, just consider what role your desires, plans, or timing have played in how you approach waiting.

Psalm 40 helps us wait patiently by resetting our expectations.

Mapping God's Faithfulness

There's another step in developing patience, and it requires a historical perspective. When you read Psalm 40, most of the verses reflect on the past. Even though the circumstances that led to its writing were intense and urgent, David emphasizes God's past help in waiting. He's not just remembering. He's memorializing God's previous deliverance. To wait patiently, we need to understand the wisdom of this focus. It's instructive.

This orientation is evident throughout the psalm, and it begins in the first three verses:

> I waited patiently for the LORD;
>> he inclined to me and heard my cry.
> He drew me up from the pit of destruction,
>> out of the miry bog,
> and set my feet upon a rock,
>> making my steps secure.
> He put a new song in my mouth,
>> a song of praise to our God. (Ps. 40:1–3a)

It's not clear what specific moment in the past David is referencing, but it's apparent that he's previously experienced God's trustworthiness in a time of fearful uncertainty. He memorializes God's track record. Eugene Peterson connects mapping God's faithfulness with an intentional strategy for perseverance. This is how we wait patiently:

> God sticks to his relationship. He establishes a personal relationship with us and stays with it. The central reality for Christians is the personal, unalterable, persevering commitment God makes to us. Perseverance is not the result of *our* determination; it is the result of God's faithfulness. We survive in the way of faith not because we have extraordinary stamina but because God is righteous, because God sticks with us. Christian discipleship is a process of paying more and more attention to God's righteousness and less and less attention to our own; finding the meaning of our lives not by probing our moods and motives and morals but by believing in God's will and purposes; making a map of the faithfulness of God, not charting the rise and fall of our enthusiasms. It is out of such a reality that we acquire perseverance.[3]

What would a map of God's faithfulness look like in your life? That question is most important when you're walking through a season of uncertainty. Those are the times when it's critical to consider how God has been with you, how he's helped you, and how your waiting hasn't been a waste.

Along with numerous journals, I have a Bible that I used for my personal devotional time over several years. After underlining a meaningful verse, I often wrote the date and a particular event next to it. Most of the time, these notes were recorded during seasons

3. Eugene H. Peterson, *A Long Obedience in the Same Direction: Discipleship in an Instant Society*, commemorative ed. (Downers Grove, IL: InterVarsity Press, 2019), 126–27.

of waiting. At the time, writing the notes was a way to reorient my heart, but now the notes serve as a memorial of God's trustworthiness. When I flip through the pages, I'm reminded how God helped me. I can trace his purposes and his plan with a historical view. The urgency of time and the tension of uncertainty don't cloud my perspective. I can see the highways and landmarks of his faithfulness.

The intensity of waiting tends to create forgetfulness. Fear, anxiety, and impatience cause us to act out of unbelief. Perhaps it would be helpful for you to pause right now and map God's faithfulness in your past. Think about a scenario where you waited longer than you expected, but where you also experienced God's provision and help. It's easy to forget these important moments. Write out a few ways that God "drew you up" and "set your feet upon a rock." How did he give you grace with the emotional challenges? What new song did the Lord help you to sing? If you like to journal, maybe it's time to go back and review the struggles of the past to highlight God's presence and care. I created a worksheet in the appendix to give you some direction if you need some assistance. This is simply a place to tangibly chronicle the situations in your life where God proved himself and an opportunity to capture the lessons that you need to rehearse.

Mapping God's faithfulness fuels waiting patiently.

Praying Imaginatively

The final encouragement for waiting patiently relates to prayer and our faith-filled imagination. By this I mean our ability to dream about what we need and desire God to do. Prayer is the venue for these future-oriented and hopeful longings. There are two places in Psalm 40 where this is expressed.

As for you, O Lord, you will not restrain
    your mercy from me;
your steadfast love and your faithfulness will
    ever preserve me. . . .

But may all who seek you
    rejoice and be glad in you;
may those who love your salvation
    say continually, "Great is the Lord!" (Ps. 40:11, 16)

If you look at other verses near these creatively hopeful prayers, you'll find honest struggle and the acknowledgment of uncertainty and pain. In verse 12 David describes so much evil surrounding him that he's lost count. In another verse (v. 14), he expresses alarm about people desiring to harm him. But he counters these realities with imaginative prayer. He looks to another realm, an other-worldly resource to be brought to him. The same message is found in Psalm 27. It's full of faith while facing false witnesses and violence.

I believe that I shall look upon the goodness of the Lord
    in the land of the living!
Wait for the Lord;
    be strong, and let your heart take courage;
    wait for the Lord! (vv. 13–14)

Since waiting is expressed twice in this psalm, it seems we could consider it another example of the call for perseverance in waiting.

It's not a violation of patience to pray with faith-filled imagination regarding what you desire God to do. Sometimes I confuse

PATIENTLY

patience with resigned acceptance. But patient waiting is not fatalistic or pessimistic. It's the hopeful commitment to seek God's help creatively and faithfully while staying put.

Instead of dreaming about what you could be doing instead of waiting or how much better your life would be without this challenge, use your imagination to fuel your faith. Page through the psalms and look for promises, assurances, or faith-filled statements. Make them your own. Talk to God about them as true as they really are. Bring the promises into your life. Imagine yourself years in the future with a hard season behind you. What do you hope will be true of you? Dream about what kind of person you'll be because of the lessons learned. It's easy to spend a lot of time thinking about what isn't happening. But patient waiting embraces what could happen *in* us more than what's happening *to* us. It looks away from circumstances to the hopeful possibility of God's gracious intervention. Andrew Murray says, "Let us therefore cultivate the habit of waiting on God, not only for what we think we need, but for all His grace and power are ready to do for us."[4]

Praying imaginatively dreams about the good outcomes of patiently waiting on God.

Cultivating Patience

Now that we've walked through some critical principles from Psalm 40, let's make this practical and personal. If you are walking through a season that is leading you to feel frustrated, anxious, or impatient, here are some steps that can help.

4. Andrew Murray, *Waiting on God! Daily Messages for a Month* (New York: Revell, 1896), 68.

1. Name Your Expectations

Part of the challenge with our expectations is that we often don't realize we have them. They can exist simply as an accepted reality without ever being challenged. Expectations can remain in the background while exerting significant emotional influence on us because they are often connected to hopes, desires, and dreams.

Naming your expectations is the practice of simply bringing to the surface what you are thinking and feeling. For example, it might sound like, "I expected to be married by forty," or, "I thought I would have heard from my boss in three weeks," or, "I hoped that we'd be parents after five years of trying to conceive," or, "I can't believe it's taking a week to get the test results back." This step helps by acknowledging the disappointment and specifically identifying the length of time we anticipated.

I've found this to be helpful, because it takes something inherently emotional and provides a way of looking at it rationally. Sometimes the length of time I've been waiting is unusually or surprisingly long. However, it's also true that my disappointment makes the waiting feel longer or more unusual than it should. Impatience and expectations tend to be unhelpful collaborators. In fact, if you look back to the examples I listed in the previous paragraph, take note of the verbs: *expected, thought, hoped,* and *believe.*

The most obvious way to apply this is when you are struggling with waiting. But I've also found it helpful to name my expectations before a potential waiting opportunity. It could sound like this: "I'm expecting this to be resolved by _____," or, "I'm assuming I'll have an answer in _____," or, "I think there will be clarity by _____." Identifying my expectations in advance provides an opportunity for me to evaluate if they are reasonable, and it serves as a reminder about the need to prepare for waiting.

Naming our expectations empowers us to face and commit them to the Lord.

2. Embrace the Tension

The second suggestion involves changing your attitude or perspective about the tension that waiting creates. Hopefully you're starting to sense a shift in how you think about waiting as you've read this book so far. I've suggested that most of us have an inherently negative view of waiting. But when you begin to see the spiritual opportunity, that can begin to change.

Patience is created as we value what God is doing in our life through the tension.

This is where mapping God's historical faithfulness is particularly helpful. By memorializing the past, we can observe how seasons of waiting were used by God for our development and growth. No doubt these times were challenging, and they may have felt pointless in the moment, but with the benefit of time we can chart the spiritual benefits. The prophet Jeremiah wrote the following in Lamentations 3:

> The LORD is good to those who wait for him,
>   to the soul who seeks him.
> It is good that one should wait quietly
>   for the salvation of the LORD.
> It is good for a man that he bear
>   the yoke in his youth. (vv. 25–27)

This may be why impatience is often associated with younger people. They usually do not have the life experience to demonstrate the value of waiting. Experience is a good teacher.

Therefore, one of the key steps in cultivating patience is embracing the tension as something good and helpful even though it's uncomfortable. This is easy to miss because our disappointment can overrule. C. S. Lewis says, "It seems to me that we often, sulkily, reject the good that God offers us because, at the moment, we expected some other good."[5] I've found it useful to remind myself of this reality by praying the following:

Lord, remind me that you are working while I'm waiting.

Jesus, I'm trusting that this tension is creating long-lasting fruit in my life.

Father, I'm releasing my right to know when this is going to end.

God, I'm believing that in waiting there's a promise of strength.

In Psalm 40, embracing the tension sounds like this: "I am poor and needy, but the LORD takes thought for me" (Ps. 40:17). Patience is formed by embracing the tension of waiting.

3. Practice Daily Waiting

The third suggestion for cultivation is a daily practice. You may have picked up this book because you are in a challenging season

5. C. S. Lewis, *Letters to Malcom: Chiefly on Prayer* (San Diego: Harcourt, 1992), 25.

right now. I hope that what you've read so far is helping to shift your perspective from what you don't know about your life to what you know to be true about God.

However, this final step seeks to create a regular rhythm that cultivates patience before it's desperately needed. I've found there's a direct relationship between this step and success in waiting because it orients my heart to a position of being "waiting ready" or "waiting aware." Andrew Murray describes it this way:

> Our private and public prayer are our chief expression of our relation to God: it is in them chiefly that our waiting upon God must be exercised. . . . Bow quietly before God, just to remember and realize who He is, how near He is, how certainly He can and will help. Just be still before Him and allow His Holy Spirit to waken and stir up in your soul the child-like disposition of absolute dependence and confident expectation. Wait upon God as a Living Being, as the Living God, who notices you, and is just longing to fill you with His salvation.[6]

In my spiritual history, I was taught to have a "quiet time." This usually involved a time for devotional reading, journaling, and the prayer form of ACTS (adoration, confession, thanksgiving, and supplication). I'm thankful for this basic spiritual discipline because it's proven beneficial to my soul. But I also found it helpful to shift my quiet time to "waiting time," the daily cultivation of patience by waiting on the Lord. Below is an overview of how I apply FAST (focus, adore, seek, and trust).

6. Murray, *Waiting on God!*, 24, 31.

Focus

- Find a quiet place where I can pray and reflect without distraction.
- Light a candle as a reminder that God is with me.
- Spend a few minutes in silent reflection, focusing my mind and slowing down my heart to embrace the importance of this moment.

Adore

- Slowly read or recite a few verses from the "Lord Is . . . " or "Lord, You Are . . . " list.
- Prayerfully meditate on what is true about God and praise him for who he is.
- Meditatively read a psalm and look for statements that can become a means of worship.

Seek

- Devotionally read a passage of Scripture, looking for promises to claim and allowing the Spirit to use the word to speak to me.
- Prayerfully review the day ahead, anticipating the ways I will need to wait on the Lord.

Trust

- Affirm my need for the Lord's help with the issues I'm wrestling with.
- Conclude by expressing hopeful trust in God: "You are going to help me."

This practice could be brief and just a few minutes. Sometimes I linger in God's presence, allowing the assurance of his help to wash over me, calm my anxiety, and bring rest to my soul. On other occasions, I find a prayer walk to be a helpful venue to shift my focus. By engaging my body, it's remarkable how I'm able to slow down, focus my prayers, and intentionally meditate. Hurry and worry tend to go together in me. Another practice is locational. There's a large park near my home, and it's a sacred space for me. The Lord and I have talked about a lot on the winding trails of the dense woods. There's something about this place and its personal history that create a natural motivation to wait on God. Sometimes it feels like I have more air in my lungs as I drive into this beautiful park. My soul seems at rest.

As you think about steps that you could take, consider building on the spiritual disciplines that minister to your soul. Perhaps you could add a few minutes to your prayer time, connecting to what you know to be true about God. Pull out your calendar and commit your activities to the Lord, praying about situations in which you'll need to wait on him. Memorize a few verses or "God is . . . " statements so that you have them available when fear or anxiety strikes. Find your sacred space and schedule some uninterrupted time to wait on the Lord.

This intentional shift from quiet time to waiting time has helped me embrace patient waiting as a lifestyle, not merely as a response to difficult situations. This daily practice resets my expectations that often make waiting harder.

Making time for intentional waiting creates a deeper reservoir of patience.

I still smile when I think about my misguided belief that I had no expectations. I've come to see the connection between my impatience and what I thought my life would look like. By redefining patience, addressing my expectations, and embracing the tension, I've experienced the strength promised in Isaiah:

> They who wait for the LORD shall renew their strength;
> they shall mount up with wings like eagles;
> they shall run and not be weary;
> they shall walk and not faint. (Isa. 40:31)

The more I've explored this cultivated patience, the more freedom I've discovered. Waiting is still hard, but this strategy has proven helpful.

I waited and waited and waited on the Lord.

It's often not what I expected, but it's good.

Reflection Questions

1. What kind of expectations for life do you have?

2. In your own words, how would you define *patience*?

3. If you haven't already, list your experience with God's faithfulness in seasons of waiting. How are you different today because of these moments?

4. Make a list of the things you hope God will do in your life because of having to wait. If you are comfortable, consider sharing this with a friend or small group.

5. Which of the three suggestions for cultivating patience are most helpful to you and why?

6. What is one action step you need to take in light of this chapter?

5

Intentionally

Waiting Is Commanded

Wait for the LORD;
be strong, and let your heart take courage;
wait for the LORD!

PSALM 27:14

"DON'T BE AFRAID. Stand still and see the salvation of the Lord."

Nearly thirty years ago, an older, godly woman looked me square in the eyes as she tried to speak, even push, this biblical truth into my anxious heart. Her timely reminder of Exodus 14:13 was needed.

I was in the middle of a senior pastor–candidacy process with my first church. Like most pastoral searches, it was complicated. I had joined the staff a year earlier, and then the senior pastor announced that he was taking a call to another church. I was asked to prayerfully interview for the role. The process was slow. Even though the search team did a commendable job, rumors circulated, and people took sides. It was messy as the process spanned several months. That's why this older woman encouraged me to patiently wait.

However, quoting Exodus 14 wasn't her only advice. She also gave me my first copy of Andrew Murray's *Waiting on God.* It spoke into my life. While I struggled to be patient, Murray showed me how to make waiting on God a choice, and how it leads to peace:

> Let us resolve at once that it shall be the one characteristic of our life and worship, a continual, humble, truthful waiting upon God. We may rest assured that He who made us for Himself, that He might give Himself to us and in us, that *He* will never disappoint us. In waiting on Him we shall find rest and joy and strength and the supply of every need.[1]

Murray's short devotionals shifted my focus from what I didn't know about my future to what I knew to be true about God. Eventually the church voted to call me as their senior pastor, and I served there for over a decade. The long season of uncertainty forced me to make the daily choice to wait on God. It was a hard but valuable lesson.

I only wish I had learned it more completely.

As I look back on my life, it seems I often don't wait intentionally. Most of my waiting happens by accident or with some degree of reluctance. Much of this book has explored unexpected uncertainty and what we do with the gaps of life. But this chapter examines choosing to wait. Instead of seeing waiting on God as

1. Andrew Murray, *Waiting on God! Daily Messages for a Month* (New York: Revell, 1896), 28.

what we do when we've tried everything else, I'd like to see if we can make waiting intentional.

Not only do we need to wait the right way; we also need to wait right away.

Waiting as a Command

From the beginning of this book, I've suggested that waiting on God relates to what or who we look to for help when facing uncertainty. Our goal is to learn how to live on what we know to be true about God when we don't know what's true about our lives. However, this is more than a suggestion.

The Bible commands it.

Psalm 27 concludes with a strong exhortation: "Wait for the LORD; be strong, and let your heart take courage; wait for the LORD!" (v. 14). The command to "wait for the LORD" is repeated twice for emphasis. What's more, it's matched with two other statements: "be strong" and "let your heart take courage." These phrases are not passive. To be strong means to have an inner confidence, to believe, or to be faithful to God's commands, and taking courage captures the idea of proving one's strength (see Josh. 23:6; Judg. 7:11; Dan. 10:19).[2]

Waiting on God is linked to spiritual empowerment.

It isn't merely what Christians do when they're stuck and powerless. It's what they do because of its close connection to hope. You can see this theme throughout the psalm. The command in Psalm 27:14 is the conclusion of a song full of confidence. David highlights that the Lord is "my light and my salvation . . . the stronghold of my life" (v. 1). He expresses confidence that

2. Ingrid Spellnes Faro, "Strength," in *Lexham Theological Wordbook*, ed. Douglas Mangum et al., Lexham Bible Reference Series (Bellingham, WA: Lexham Press, 2014).

his enemies will be defeated (v. 2), and he will not give in to fear despite overwhelming odds (v. 3). There's also a priority of worship as David articulates his singular passion: to dwell in the house of the Lord, gazing upon God's beauty (v. 4).

At the same time, not everything is clear and simple. David is still concerned about unanswered prayers (v. 7). He worries about God's disposition toward him and the fear of being forsaken (vv. 8–9). He's experienced rejection by his family (v. 10). People are lying about him (v. 12). This background and setting are important to understand. The gaps in David's life are many and ongoing.

That's why the final command to wait is so powerful.

Waiting on God is a choice to face uncertainty differently. Since waiting means to look to something, this command involves the choice to look to God—who he is, what we know about him, his gracious history—to fill the spaces that tend to attract our fear, anxiety, or frustration. Let that sink in for a second. This could be a major shift in your thinking.

Here's what I mean: instead of seeing waiting as something that happens *to* you, I'd like you to see waiting as something you *choose* to do. Rather than seeing waiting as what to do when you are stuck, what if you intentionally embraced it? What if waiting on the Lord is an expression of obedience? What if it's an act of hope-filled, gutsy faith? For many of us (myself included), this could be deeply transformational.

Living with unfulfilled desires, unmet needs, and unclear answers, we can slip into a pattern in which we feel out of control and confused. The lack of purpose in these seasons can lead to frustration. Our inability to control circumstances can create persistent patterns of anxiety. In this way, it's easy to see how waiting can be wasted.

But it's all a matter of perspective.

There are moments in life that are wonderfully intentional when it comes to waiting. Take a wedding as an example. While Christian weddings have a lot of variety, there's one moment they all share. It's my favorite: the entrance of the bride. As an officiant for many weddings, I've had a great purview of the bridesmaids completing their entrance and the pause before the bride walks down the aisle. It's a beautiful moment as the mother of the bride stands along with friends and family. But prior to this regal walk, everyone in the room is waiting. And without complaint.

To be invited to a wedding requires that you come early enough to be seated and wait for the bride to enter. The space between being ushered to your seat and the start of the wedding is not only expected; it's also part of what it means to attend a wedding. While no one says it directly, "be seated and wait" is what guests do.

Waiting for a bride isn't a waste. It's expected. It's required. And the same could be said about Christians. Waiting is what Christians are supposed to do.

Waiting for the Lord is a command that we obey.

Waiting as Identity

Psalm 27 isn't the only place we see an intentional shift in perspective. Other texts help us see that waiting is an apt descriptor of who we are. It's our identity. Christians are those who wait.

We find this theme repeated in Psalm 31. You're probably familiar with the fifth verse because Jesus famously quoted it in the final moments of his life: "Into your hand I commit my spirit" (v. 5). But it's the final verse that contains the waiting theme: "Be strong, and let your heart take courage, all you who wait for the

Lord" (v. 24). Once again, it's the concluding statement after a series of verses expressing concern about the need for protection, deliverance, guidance, and comfort.

The themes are similar to Psalm 27 with one exception. Rather than merely issuing a command, Psalm 31 uses waiting for the Lord as a statement of identity. The ones who are commanded to be strong and courageous are those who wait for the Lord (v. 24). The psalm is just as filled with hope: "Oh, how abundant is your goodness, which you have stored up for those who fear you and worked for those who take refuge in you" (v. 19). But the intentional posture is slightly different.

Waiting for the Lord characterizes those who hope in the Lord. It's who we are.

Eugene Peterson combines hope, waiting, and identity with the biblical role of a watchman. This person's task is to fix his eyes on the horizon and wait. Looking for something yet to arrive, especially danger, is essential to the security of a city. Long gaps of time would not have been a surprise. To be a watchman is to wait. Here's how Peterson says it:

> The words *wait* and *hope* are connected with the image of a watchman waiting through the night for the dawn. The connection provides important insights for the person in trouble who cries out, "But surely there is something for me to do!" The answer is yes, there is something for you to do, or more exactly there is someone you can *be:* be a watchman.[3]

3. Eugene H. Peterson, *A Long Obedience in the Same Direction: Discipleship in an Instant Society*, commemorative ed. (Downers Grove: InterVarsity Press, 2019), 136.

I find that to be a helpful category. Being a watchman involves both a required task and a role to embrace. It's hard to imagine a watchman complaining about all the waiting, because it's an essential part of the job. Psalm 31 speaks to "all you who wait for the LORD" (v. 24). That's a description summarizing other references throughout the psalm, such as "those who fear you and . . . those who take refuge in you" (v. 19) and "all you his saints" (v. 23).

Waiting on the Lord means intentionally embracing our identity as waiters. Think of it as moving from "I have to wait" to "Waiting is what I'm supposed to do." Or maybe taking it a step further: "Waiting on God is an expression of who I am."

Christians wait.

I remember years ago reading Dallas Willard's book *Renovation of the Heart*. At the time I had a rather limited view of God's grace. I saw it as mainly applying to salvation and the forgiveness of sins. Willard helped me expand my view of grace to apply to any way in which I need God's help and empowerment. He said that it's not just the ungodly who need grace, but the godly need it too.

> The greatest saints are not those who need less grace but those who consume the most grace, who indeed are most in need of grace, those who are saturated by grace in every dimension of their being. Grace to them is like breath.[4]

The idea of breathing grace was helpful to my soul and the process of sanctification in my life. I think the same thing is true for waiting.

4. Dallas Willard, *Renovation of the Heart: Putting on the Character of Christ* (Colorado Springs, CO: NavPress, 2002), 93–94.

Waiting is not just what Christians do. It's who we are—an essential identity marker of what it means to be a follower of Jesus. We'll explore this further in the next chapter as we consider how to wait together. But for now, I hope that you are starting to realize that we need to change how we think about waiting and how we approach it.

Choose to Wait

If we are going to embrace waiting as a choice, we need to consider the different kinds of waiting. There are three unique opportunities where we can make this intentional choice.

1. Responding

When gaps emerge in our lives, we don't know what to do. Unanswered questions and delayed resolutions can lead to unique temptations. In my experience, this is where most of us start. These are the kinds of moments that are easy to waste. I'm sure you're familiar with this scenario. It may be the reason you've picked up this book.

I hope that you are now empowered to embrace the opportunity to wait. Rather than resenting and resisting the position you're in, you could see it as an opportunity for spiritual transformation. Instead of constantly mulling over what isn't clear or known, consider intentionally rehearsing the following:

- Waiting is normal and hard. I shouldn't be surprised.
- God is in control of the events and the timing of my life. I can rest.
- There's a lot I know to be true about God right now. I should think about that.

- This uncertainty pushes me to dependent prayer. That's really good.
- I can draw upon the Lord's strength. He promises to help me when I wait.

Even as I've written this book, I've noticed a shift in how I respond to delays and uncertainty. I'm less shocked and annoyed by them. Don't get me wrong—they're still hard. I hate living with the tension of not knowing what's going on. But I'm finding that a simple shift in perspective and making the choice to embrace my waiting has been helpful.

I'm making the choice to respond and not react.

2. Preparing

The second scenario embraces waiting as more than an event. It applies the truths of Psalms 27 and 31 by seeing waiting as a vital part of the Christian life. If it's central to being a follower of Jesus, then it should be expected and anticipated. It should be studied. We should consider how to prepare to wait.

I remember hearing John Piper say that the time to prepare your people for suffering is before they suffer. Christian discipleship should involve a theology of hardship, but that's hard to develop when you are in the middle of it. The same is true about waiting. The time to develop a theology of waiting is before you're living in "gap land."

How could you anticipate waiting? After you've begun to change your perspective on where it fits in the Christian life, you could take further steps by looking in the Bible at all the direct and indirect references to waiting. I've included a list for the book of Psalms in appendix 4. Another step would be to add waiting to your regular prayer list: "Lord, I'm sure to encounter moments today when I need to wait." I've added a short section like this in my regular prayer time. This is especially important when my anxiety is high. After quieting my heart, I slowly recite and meditate on verses that remind me about God's character. Or I pray over the spiritual armor in Ephesians 6, reflecting on the resources God has given me. Remember, waiting on God is simply looking to him. With that in mind, I'll frequently pray, "God, I'm waiting on you." Additionally, you might consider memorizing a few key verses so that they become ingrained in your thinking and quickly recalled when needed. Take time to rehearse them—slowly and meditatively. Finally, I've found that Andrew Murray's daily meditations help shape my perspective. His classic book provides short encouragement on the value of waiting on God.

Since waiting on God is commanded and therefore integral to our Christian identity, it's vital to find ways to put it into practice on a regular basis. The small—even daily—practice of waiting gets us ready for longer and more intense seasons.

Take time to prepare to wait.

3. Planning

The third scenario of intentional waiting involves planning. I don't mean that we expect it to happen. We've addressed that issue previously. Rather, this step involves factoring waiting on the Lord into our decision-making. It makes room for it because it's a vital part of decisions or actions.

We need to plan our waiting.

In this step, we move toward a more proactive approach. If we've come to value waiting, then it will make sense to build it into more aspects of our lives. Consider what it would look like if you planned for a few days to wait on the Lord before making a decision. What if churches had committed times of waiting before moving forward on a new initiative? Imagine a strategic plan that included waiting as a vital part of its process or implementation. Again I'm reminded, when I look back on my life and ministry, that waiting on the Lord is not something I've embraced intentionally. It's usually a reaction toward a hindrance, delay, or challenge.

But if waiting on God is that important, we should plan for it.

As I've worked on this book, I've noticed a change in how I approach decisions. As I've developed my understanding and affection for waiting on the Lord, I'm making decisions, responding to emails, or even offering my opinion more slowly. Instead of allowing anxiety or fear to push me into quick action, I've marveled at how helpful it is to take a few days to wait upon God. It's amazing to me how creating space has been helpful. By focusing my heart on him, slowing down my thoughts, meditating on Scripture, and talking to God about the issue, there's often an unusual level of clarity. Even if the solution is not as evident as I'd like, waiting on God has created deeper levels of peace in me.

My attitude is changing when it comes to waiting.

I can hardly believe it!

Sometimes I've even witnessed the Lord solving the issue or providing an alternative before I take any action. That's what Isaiah 64:4 says: "No eye has seen a God besides you, who acts for those who wait for him." There are times when God directly intervenes as we wait on him. So before I speak or act quickly, I need to factor waiting on God into the mix.

As I plan to wait, I've seen God work!

I'm sure I read the following paragraph from Andrew Murray over thirty years ago. It lands on me differently today:

> Let [waiting] become so much our consciousness that the utterance comes spontaneously, "On Thee *I do wait* all the day; *I wait* on Thee." This will indeed imply sacrifice and separation, a soul entirely given up to God as its all, its only joy. This waiting on God has hardly yet been acknowledged as the only true Christianity. And yet, if it be true that God alone is goodness and joy and love; if it be true that our highest blessedness is in having as much of God as we can; if it be true that Christ has redeemed us wholly for God, and made a life of continual abiding in His presence possible, nothing less ought to satisfy than to be ever breathing this blessed atmosphere, "I wait on Thee."[5]

In preparation for a funeral for the woman who encouraged me with Exodus 14, I reviewed my journal during my candidacy at my first church. It was a remarkable journey to see how the Lord worked in my life and in our church. Daily entries were filled with spiritual lessons, but they weren't easy at the time. Waiting on the Lord was hard. But there's no question about the value and fruit. Looking back now, I can see the value of that season. I wouldn't have chosen to wait on the Lord if it were up to me. But the more

5. Murray, *Waiting on God!*, 44.

I learn about waiting, and the more I see its spiritual benefits, the more inclined I am to intentionally wait.

We not only need to wait the right way; we need to wait right away—intentionally.

Reflection Questions

1. How has your perspective or attitude changed since picking up this book?

2. How could seeing waiting as a command and as your identity practically help you not to waste your waiting?

3. Reflect on the three opportunities to choose to wait. Which of the three is most challenging to you and why?

4. Identify one or two practical steps for preparing to wait. Write them out in detail and share them with a friend or small group.

5. Can you think of a circumstance in your life that would benefit from planning to wait?

6

Collectively

Waiting Is Relational

*He presented himself alive to them after his suffering
by many proofs, appearing to them during forty days
and speaking about the kingdom of God. And while
staying with them he ordered them not to depart from
Jerusalem, but to wait for the promise of the Father.*

ACTS 1:3–4

EVERY CHRISTIAN IS WAITING.

Most of us consider this reality from a personal vantage point.
We individualize it. That may be the reason you picked up this
book. Perhaps there's something in your life that you desire, but
it's been delayed. Or maybe there are painful circumstances that
you long to see resolved, but you're living in tension. Hopefully,
the previous chapters helped you embrace a different attitude and
practice a better strategy with waiting.

This personal perspective is a good starting point. It's where my journey began. I sensed a deep longing to grow in my understanding of waiting on God. As I've wrestled through the writing of each chapter, I've grown in my appreciation of this biblical practice. I'm more convinced than ever that waiting on God is essential for my spiritual growth. I hope you are seeing this to be true in your life and coming to the same conclusion.

A Collective Vision

However, through my research, I realized that I wasn't thinking broadly enough. I discovered something that I didn't consider at the beginning of my journey: Christians wait on God together. There's something collective about waiting. Whether we realize it or not, we're all waiting on God. At some level, every Christian is in the same position. While there may be different circumstances, intensities, or challenges, every Christian is presently living in some "gap land." Waiting on God is the biblical and transformative baseline for the entire church. As a result, there's an opportunity to help each other as we wait. Andrew Murray stokes the fire of this vision when he writes:

> Oh! what will not the Church be able to do when her individual members learn to live their lives waiting on God, and when together, with all of self and the world sacrificed in the fire of love, they unite in waiting with one accord for the promise of the Father, once so gloriously fulfilled, but still unexhausted.[1]

---

1. Andrew Murray, *Waiting on God! Daily Messages for a Month* (New York: Revell, 1896), 138.

One way we waste our waiting is by not realizing that God invites us to pursue it with other people, to integrate waiting into the normal life of the body of Christ. This chapter seeks to explore this collective vision and how we might apply a holistic perspective in several familiar areas.

We need to wait on God together.

The Church Began by Waiting

Let's start with the birth of the church.

After the resurrection, one of Jesus's earliest commands to his disciples was for them to wait. However, it's easy to miss this simple truth and its importance. Yet this is the context in which the church began and the Spirit was poured out. In Acts 1:3–5, Luke records these instructions from Jesus:

> He presented himself alive to them after his suffering by many proofs, appearing to them during forty days and speaking about the kingdom of God. And while staying with them he ordered them not to depart from Jerusalem, but to wait for the promise of the Father, which, he said, "you heard from me; for John baptized with water, but you will be baptized with the Holy Spirit not many days from now." (Acts 1:3–5)

Take note that Jesus commanded the disciples to wait. Can you imagine the tension? They must have been alarmed, wondering if Roman or Jewish leaders were looking for them. Yet their first orders from the resurrected Messiah were to wait and not flee the danger. Apparently the disciples weren't thrilled with this instruction because they inquired about the next steps in the plan of

God. Jesus rather bluntly redirected their question and reframed their future role:

> He said to them, "It is not for you to know times or seasons that the Father has fixed by his own authority. But you will receive power when the Holy Spirit has come upon you, and you will be my witnesses in Jerusalem and in all Judea and Samaria, and to the end of the earth." (Acts 1:7–8)

Just think about these two texts. Uncertainty, tension, and waiting are how the church began. Forty days later as the disciples were waiting together, the Holy Spirit arrived with flames of fire over their heads. They began to speak in other tongues (Acts 2:4). Peter preached his famous sermon when about three thousand people were converted (Acts 2:41). You may be familiar with this story. It's the amazing launch of the church.

But there was also a lot of waiting.

I wonder how many Christians think about the mission of the church in this way. If you just read the Great Commission in Matthew 28, it sounds active: "Go . . . make disciples, baptizing them . . . teaching them to observe" (Matt. 28:19–20). But this mission activity also involves a lot of waiting on God. It practically looks like this: wait and go and wait and go.

Waiting on God is vital to the mission of God.

Waiting is how the church began!

The Church Continued to Wait

Miraculous power and fruitfulness characterized the early church. Reading the book of Acts, we get a sense of the activity, progress, and even the opposition. But we shouldn't miss the critical moments of waiting. Here are a few examples:

- After Peter and John's arrest and being threatened by the religious leaders, the church waited together, praying for wisdom, protection, and empowerment. (Acts 4:23–31)

- Jesus appeared to Saul on the Damascus road and told him, "Rise and enter the city, and you will be told what you are to do." He waited three days for the arrival of Ananias and the recovery of his sight. (Acts 9:6–19)

- When Peter was imprisoned by Herod during the Passover, the church waited with earnest prayer to God, and it's the first place Peter visits after his miraculous release. (Acts 12:1–19)

- During Paul and Silas's imprisonment in Philippi, they turned their jail cell into a place of worship while they waited for God's miraculous deliverance. (Acts 16:16–34)

It's instructive that many memorable moments of the early church are connected to waiting on God. We tend to focus on the activity and advancement of the gospel, but it's important to remember the context of tension-filled gaps. Seeking God in the middle of uncertainty is a familiar theme for those who embrace the call of God.

As I look at the landscape of Christianity and the activity of the church, I don't see a lot of emphasis on waiting. Instead, there's a high premium placed on action, movement, growth, and expansion. Don't get me wrong—I heartily believe in the Great Commission and evangelism. Seeing the kingdom of God advance and the hearts of people change brings me incredible joy. But I wonder if our individual struggle with waiting is partly because it's unfamiliar in the regular life of the church.

Waiting isn't just essential for Christians; it's essential for the entire church in every generation.

The Church Is Still Waiting

"Come, Lord Jesus!"

This statement is part of the final two verses of Revelation. It reflects the concluding passion of those who read the last book of the Bible carefully. Everything in its twenty-two chapters is designed to create a longing for the second coming of Jesus Christ. Revelation is written so that Christians will live with an understanding about "the things that must soon take place" (Rev. 1:1) and to inspire endurance through times of difficulty (14:12). Nancy Guthrie, in *Blessed: Experiencing the Promise of the Book of Revelation*, highlights the centrality of waiting in this final book: "Revelation is a call to patient endurance of tribulation as we await the coming of Christ's kingdom in all of its fullness."[2] In other words, the last biblical book isn't merely about events in the future. Revelation helps God's people as they wait together.

Throughout the New Testament, the biblical writers pick up this waiting theme as a motivator not only for patience but also for godliness. A biblical understanding of waiting creates

2. Nancy Guthrie, *Blessed: Experiencing the Promise of the Book of Revelation* (Wheaton, IL: Crossway, 2022), 145.

an opportunity for collective spiritual growth. Peter makes this connection in his second epistle:

> Since all these things are thus to be dissolved, what sort of people ought you to be in lives of holiness and godliness, waiting for and hastening the coming of the day of God, because of which the heavens will be set on fire and dissolved, and the heavenly bodies will melt as they burn! But according to his promise we are waiting for new heavens and a new earth in which righteousness dwells. (2 Pet. 3:11–13)

Do you understand what Peter is saying? When Christians properly embrace a biblical view of waiting, it creates an invitation to more spiritual maturity and godliness. It reminds us that we're not supposed to be living for the kingdom of this world. We're waiting for another kingdom. It calls us to live not for immediate satisfaction but the approval of our coming King. It challenges us to not take revenge or become bitter because a future judgment awaits. And it reinforces the limitations of our strength as we embrace the need for God's help.

The challenge is that we forget this. That's why we need others to help us. One of my pastoral survival strategies is to regularly give a friend in ministry a call. It's helpful to talk about the challenges, seek advice, and just have someone who understands the difficulties of pastoral ministry. On one call, I was pretty discouraged. Sensing my weariness, my friend concluded our conversation by rehearsing the gospel to me and then saying, "It won't be long, brother." Hearing the central truth that defines my life along with an exhortation about the future was strangely helpful. It reminded me of what I believed (knew to be true about God), and it reset my perspective on how I was viewing my life. While he didn't use the word *wait*, it's certainly what he had in mind. His words remind me of what Andrew Murray said:

> Strengthen and encourage each other in the holy exercise of waiting, that each may not only say of it himself, but of his brethren, "We have waited for Him; we will be glad and rejoice in His salvation."[3]

We need to remind each other that we're still waiting. We need to encourage each other as we wait.

Four Ways to Help Each Other Wait

We're not the only ones waiting, and it's important to consider how to help each other during these challenging seasons. It's easy to become discouraged and exhausted as we live in a lingering delay. But there's something powerful and helpful in waiting together. What are some ways that we can encourage each other?

Preparation

In the previous chapter, I said that the time to develop a biblical understanding of waiting is before it begins. That's true on a personal level as you prayerfully anticipate events, meetings, or expectations that may present opportunities to wait. However, I have something much broader in mind here.

3. Murray, *Waiting on God!*, 58.

Given the centrality of waiting in the Christian life, it seems that we should be thinking and talking about waiting a lot more as a community. We could help each other wait more effectively if it was a theme that emerged more often in our worship services, teaching, counseling training, and in discipleship processes. Our Sunday morning gatherings could serve as weekly reminders that we're still waiting. Imagine a call to worship framed around this theme. Or we could add silence into the order of worship to create an intentional moment of waiting. Weekly worship affirms that we're still waiting together. As I've taught about waiting on God, I've been surprised how it not only resonates with my church, but how unusual it feels to people. It seems to me that we've made progress in preparing people for suffering and tragedy, but it doesn't appear that we've spent enough time developing and teaching a theology of waiting. Counseling and discipleship could be leveraged as well. Helping people navigate uncertainty, expectations, and delays is a vital part of spiritual formation. Sometimes anger and anxiety are merely the "presentation issues" of a deeper need.

Putting off frustration means putting on waiting on God.

When it comes to discipleship, I wonder if we've prioritized this issue appropriately. As we think about the process of spiritual maturity and the competencies that are needed, it seems that learning to wait should be part of our formation strategy. What's more, it's increasingly important in leadership development. After serving as a pastor for over thirty years, I've noticed that younger leaders have higher expectations for faster results and advancement. The legacy of our culture of speed is catching up with us. As I coach and mentor, I'm adding discussions on waiting into the mix because it's both needed and more foreign. Paul's final words to Timothy need to be carefully considered: "Reprove, rebuke, and exhort, with *complete patience*" (2 Tim. 4:2).

Waiting on God is so important and central to the Christian life that we should prioritize it. We help each other by preparing to wait.

Compassion

The second consideration for helping others to wait is a posture of compassion. I began this book with an obvious but important assumption: waiting is hard. While that's a good starting point for not wasting our waiting personally, it's also something to consider as we care for one another.

"Hope deferred makes the heart sick" (Prov. 13:12). Solomon captures the deep heartache of unfulfilled longings and unrelenting disappointment. Waiting can be brutal. But it's even more painful when the people around you are insensitive or uncaring about the pain. That's why I appreciate the vivid wisdom in Proverbs. Waiting isn't just hard. It can make your heart feel ill.

A small but important step in caring for one another is the simple acknowledgment that waiting is hard—really hard. The pain of delayed desires can lead to loneliness, isolation, shame, and insecurity. Sometimes the internal wrestling creates spiritual doubts or a sense of confusion: Why is this so hard? Why can't I just be content? Why isn't God answering my prayer? This is where the community plays an important, caring role.

Compassion might take on many different expressions. Sometimes it could be as simple as recognizing the difficulty and validating the struggle. Or it could look like lovingly checking in with a friend whose waiting has continued for a long time. In other situations, it might be helpful to have a conversation about how they are processing this season or what they are learning. Or there might be times where meeting tangible needs (e.g., meals, mowing a lawn, or watching their kids) provides some relief and communicates compassion. We tend to think of these expressions of love when there's a major crisis in a person's life. But waiting can also be traumatic and intense. A compassionate posture, combined with acts of kindness, is a way for us to help each other navigate the emotionally challenging waters of waiting.

Dylan and Melody know the heartbreaking journey of waiting. But they also know the power of a compassionate community. Several years ago they embraced a calling from the Lord to become foster parents, and a precious little boy, Dallas, was placed in their home. He was only sixteen months old with a tragic story, but they were determined to help. Eventually the temporary placement moved toward the possibility of adoption. However, the emotional and physical needs in their foster child's life were daunting and complicated. And the system that was supposed to protect Dallas failed him multiple times. With the hope of welcoming Dallas into their home, Dylan and Melody embraced the risk, pain, and uncertainty. But a process that should have taken months dragged on for years.

Their waiting was agonizing.

However, a kind-hearted nurse at a doctor's office witnessed their battle and introduced Dylan and Melody to a care community at her church. This unique ministry involved five couples committed to serving them through weekly meals, prayer, and childcare—simple acts of compassion. These tangible touch-points of grace fueled Dylan and Melody's endurance through the traumatic highs and lows of caring for Dallas and navigating a broken system. In reflecting on that season, they said: "Waiting is so hard. When our faith was crumbling or when deep questions were haunting us, the kindness of our care community reminded us that the Lord is with us. They were willing to step into the waiting with us even though it was messy."

After over two years and multiple court hearings, Dallas's adoption was granted. At the finalization ceremony, the courtroom was filled with people who were instrumental in helping Dylan and Melody. Family, friends, and the care community gathered to celebrate. The long journey with waiting was complete. But the story continues, because Melody launched a care community in her church that serves foster and adoptive families. Twenty-five people have already embraced the opportunity to walk alongside hurting people, and this ministry continues to grow as more people catch the vision.

Dylan and Melody know firsthand that compassionate care is one important way to help people wait.

Prayer

Biblical waiting and prayer are deeply connected. Most of the references in the psalms to waiting on God are related to either a call to pray or a posture of seeking God's help. Waiting isn't doing nothing. It's directing the heart toward who God is. Lamentations 3:25 says, "The LORD is good to those who wait for him, to the soul who seeks him." While prayer isn't specifically mentioned, it's clear that it's vital to this orientation.

One of the ways that we can help one another wait is to make this pathway between prayer and waiting more apparent, especially as we pray together. Creating prayer venues for seeking the Lord, especially for those who are waiting, is another way to help people wait. For the last fifteen years, our church has hosted a monthly prayer meeting on a Sunday evening. The attendance is rarely large, but it's created a helpful rhythm of seeking God's help. Usually we provide time in the service for individuals to receive prayer from a small group after they share about their need. The circumstances vary, but a common theme is waiting for a health need, a wayward child, a job opportunity, a pregnancy, or a meaningful relationship. As these people gather around the person in need, their prayers become fuel for endurance. We've not only witnessed God answering prayer in profound ways, but we've also marveled at how this simple ministry strengthens the faith of those who are waiting.

Since prayer and waiting are deeply connected, providing venues for intercession is another way we can help each other wait.

Encouragement

The final way that we can help one another wait is by providing specific biblical encouragement. Since waiting is hard, it's easy to allow false narratives to dominate our thinking. We become focused on what's *not* true about our lives, and we can fail to remember what *is* true about God. This is where the community of believers plays an essential role. The writer of Hebrews commands the church to intentionally exhort one another as the intensity of waiting increases.

> Let us hold fast the confession of our hope without wavering, for he who promised is faithful. And let us consider how to stir up one another to love and good works, not neglecting to meet together, as is the habit of some, but encouraging one another, and all the more as you see the Day drawing near. (Heb. 10:23–25)

This kind of encouragement can be expressed through singing, sermons, Bible studies, counseling, and discipleship conversations. The body of Christ plays a critical role in reminding us who God is, what he's like, and why he can be trusted. This must be done regularly and consistently to ward off the gravitational pull toward viewing waiting as a waste.

I've found this to be personally true. There have been times when I desperately needed to worship with other believers because their singing helped to strengthen my resolve and remind me what I believe. As corporate worship washes over me, and as I see the confidence of my fellow church members, it affects my faith. I find myself thinking, "That's right! This is true! I can trust God." I've lost count of how many times the corporate gathering of God's people has helped me wait. A simple reminder about the substance of my faith served to help me wait on the Lord another week.

One of my desires from this book is that you might not only learn how to wait on God but also become a means of encouragement to others. There may be a particular verse or a "God is . . ." statement that you'll have the opportunity to share. The Lord may be preparing you for a ministry to people with whom you share a common waiting story. Or you may be in a position of leadership or spiritual influence where you can help others in their journey through the difficult terrain of waiting.

We're all waiting, and we need each other.

A Prayer

This chapter surprised me. First, it never dawned on me to think about waiting from a collective perspective. One of the discoveries has been how I tend to individualize waiting. I was stunned to see how waiting on God is so connected to the life of the church. Second, I was surprised at how challenging it was to think about how we help each other wait. I'm not sure I've ever thought carefully about a strategy for assisting others to wait on God. So I'm sure you can think of other applications, and I hope you find your own creative way to help others as they wait.

Every Christian, at some level and in some way, is waiting.

I hope that we might be able to embrace the mindset and prayerful posture of Andrew Murray when he wrote this prayer. I hope it becomes your own. I want to make it mine:

Blessed Father! we humbly beseech Thee, Let none that wait on Thee be ashamed; no, not one. Some are weary, and the time of waiting appears long. And some are feeble, and scarcely know how to wait. And some are so entangled in the effort of their prayers and their work, they think that they can find no time to wait continually. Father! teach us all how to wait. Teach us to think of each other and pray for each other. Teach us to think of Thee, the God of all waiting ones. Father! let none that wait on Thee be ashamed. For Jesus' sake. Amen.[4]

Reflection Questions

1. Prior to this chapter, how did you think about the collective nature of waiting? What do you think informed your viewpoint?

2. How has your perspective changed?

4. Murray, *Waiting on God!*, 40.

3. Why is it important to consider waiting in the establishment and mission of the church?

4. Which of the four ways to help each other wait is most significant or applicable to you or the community in which you serve?

5. Can you think of other ways in which we might help each other?

6. Consider writing your own prayer for others and share it with some friends.

Conclusion

Embracing Our Waiting

And now, O Lord, for what do I wait?
My hope is in you.

IT PROBABLY WON'T SURPRISE YOU to learn that I'm a sunrise guy.

I'm not saying sunsets are silly. There's certainly something beautiful about watching a red and orange sun slide into the ocean as rays of light shoot into a slowly darkening sky. I've got lots of memories sitting on a blanket with family and friends as day turns to twilight. But I still prefer a sunrise, and my last name is still Vroegop. I love watching the sun pierce the morning fog or peak over a mountain as it announces the beginning of a new day. There's something fresh and hopeful about the first light. I find few things more delightful than a quiet morning, a cup of coffee, a lawn chair, and a sky lighting up with the early morning rays of sunshine.

Several years ago I dreamed of watching the sun rise over the Grand Canyon on the first day of the year. During a Christmas

CONCLUSION

vacation to Arizona, we trekked to the South Rim and reserved a hotel on New Year's Eve. I laid out a plan for the morning—where we'd go, what time we'd leave—to witness this incredible moment of beauty. Overnight a rare winter storm blanketed the region with several inches of snow, making a beautiful landscape even more stunning. I couldn't wait for the morning.

While it was still dark, and with fresh wet snow on the ground, we made our way to an observation area about thirty minutes before sunrise. Besides a few photographers, we were the only visitors, and we had our choice of the best location. My family huddled together and waited. I couldn't have been happier.

But my serene moment didn't last long.

Behind us I could hear multiple tour bus doors opening. Before we knew it, our special location was overtaken with a hundred others. Our viewing spot became obstructed, and my wife was boxed out by an aggressive photographer. My young daughter's feet were wet with snow, and she started complaining that her toes were freezing. "Can I please go back to the car?" she begged. When she started shivering, my wife said, "I'm sorry, Mark, but I need to take her back and get her warmed up. You can stay."

My dream of watching the sunrise together with family evaporated.

As I waited for the sun to rise over the Grand Canyon, I had a lot of internal tension. Disappointment that my dream didn't work out. Frustration with the crowds and my daughter's selection of shoes. Regret that I didn't plan better for the visit. My expectations for what I thought was going to be true about our Grand Canyon visit weren't met. I debated about running back to the car to see if my wife and daughter would rejoin me.

But the sun was starting to rise. I decided to wait.

As the morning rays of sunshine filled the canyon, it was breathtaking. The wintery mist evaporated in the hues of yellow, red, and orange light that shone on the deep walls of the South Rim. The canyon changed colors every few minutes as the sun penetrated deeper and deeper. It was an amazing display of beauty. I found my heart drawn to worship as my eyes beheld a scene that platformed the creative glory of God. It was an amazing experience.

But I almost missed it with wasted waiting.

As I've written this book, I've often thought about that moment as a metaphor for my journey in waiting on God. There are numerous situations that come to mind where I missed a beautiful moment because I was focused on my desires, expectations, plans, or dreams. Disappointment or frustration has often stolen my joy. Rising in front of me is a glorious opportunity, but I'm distracted with what isn't happening or what I don't know. You can miss a beautiful sunrise because your expectations aren't met.

Life is full of unplanned gap moments, and it's easy to waste them.

Redeemed Waiting

The aim of this book has been to help us wait on God by learning to live *on what we know to be true about God when we don't know what's true about our lives.* Did you notice that I changed the *you* to *we?* That's intentional, especially as we come to the conclusion. You see, I've written this book with both of us in mind. I hope you've sensed that I'm journeying with you in learning how to not waste my waiting. My vision for *Waiting Isn't a Waste* was to recapture an important biblical concept, which I sense is deficient in my life. Maybe you decided to read this book because you sensed the same thing. Or perhaps you're desperate to know how to navigate a tension-filled "gap land." Regardless, I'm thankful that you decided to explore what it means to wait on God, and I hope you'll continue learning and applying the truths of this book. I feel like I've just begun my journey. My last name still means "early up," and my bias for action hasn't diminished. I still have the same personality, tendencies, and temptations. The same is true for you. This book probably didn't fundamentally change you or your circumstances.

However, I can say that I'm wasting my waiting less.

The pervasive negative attitude I had about waiting has started to warm to it. I'm not saying that I love waiting, and I don't know if I'll ever get there. The tension implicit in delays and uncertainty is still quite uncomfortable. But I'm coming to appreciate the redemptive nature of my gap moments. I'm starting to embrace my vulnerability as an opportunity for deeper spiritual growth, to focus on who God is rather than what I don't know. Even though it's hard and common, I'm starting to approach waiting thoughtfully and patiently. I'm less surprised and frustrated by delays. Writing these chapters has helped me to miss fewer opportunities to wait on the Lord. While the struggle remains, my waiting is more intentional and less reactionary. I'm more convinced than ever that God works for those who wait for him (Isa. 64:4). I've seen it. In fact, I'm trying to find ways to help other people as they wait too.

I'm looking for more ways to embrace my waiting.

I hope that's your posture as well.

A Few Lessons

As we draw our journey to a close, I'd like to share a few of the personal lessons I've learned from writing about and considering waiting. My hope is that you'll resonate with most of them. Feel free to add your own. I can't wait to hear the stories of how readers like you started to embrace waiting on God and what they learned.

Learning to wait on God has been a surprising journey. Along the way, I learned five lessons.

1. Disdain for Waiting Is Connected to a Desire for Control

Why do I dislike waiting? That was a significant question for me as I thought about both my experience and writing this book. It was fairly easy to identify the emotions and responses: frustration, fear, anxiety, or anger. But I needed to unpack what lies underneath. I'm now convinced the issue is control. Waiting confronts my desire to be in charge of my life. Understanding what is happening, knowing the timing, and assuring an outcome make me feel secure and safe. Vulnerability is unnerving. This has helped me see gap moments as opportunities to trust in God, to embrace the safety and security of who he is and what he's promised.

Embracing waiting confronts my desire for control.

2. Waiting Isn't Getting Easier, Culturally or Personally

There's a gravitational pull away from valuing waiting, and it's not getting any better. There are significant incentives for things to happen faster, and I feel the conditioning of speed and efficiency.

Without even knowing it, my expectations have changed, and it's hard not to allow this to creep into nearly every area of my life. What's more, life experience can fuel anxiety because I have more painful examples of what could go wrong. However, realizing this tendency around me and inside of me created an empowerment to treat it like white noise. I'm able to see the struggle with waiting more clearly and not hitch my wagon to the lure of quick answers or fast solutions.

Embracing waiting requires resisting external and internal allurements.

3. Waiting on God Is Not Optional for the Christian Life

I began this journey with a desire to improve in a particular area of deficiency, but I soon discovered that waiting on God is a critical aspect of being a follower of Jesus. Andrew Murray, toward the end of his book, writes:

> Dear Christian! do you not begin to see that waiting is not one among a number of Christian virtues, to be thought of from time to time, but that it expresses that disposition which lies at the very root of the Christian life?[1]

Waiting is more like abiding. It's closer to trust and faith. It describes a normal and central element of discipleship that I cannot neglect. To be a Christian is to wait on God. Understanding this added fuel to my desire to grow in this vital area. It's transformed how I think about and value waiting.

1. Andrew Murray, *Waiting on God! Daily Messages for a Month* (New York: Revell, 1896), 116.

Embracing waiting facilitates spiritual maturity and intimacy with God.

4. Daily Waiting on God Helps Tame Reactions and Embrace Peace

I've noticed a connection between intentional waiting and my responses. You see, I still don't like waiting, and I'm not sure I will. But I've experienced a level of freedom through this journey that I want to continue. As I've embraced waiting on God as a daily discipline, it's produced some wonderful results. Taking a few minutes to focus, adore, seek, and trust has produced notable fruit. Delays are less surprising. Uncertainty is more tolerable. I'm less inclined to speak or respond quickly. I've welcomed God into many more moments of my day. I just feel less worried and stressed. My load seems lighter, and I sense a greater closeness with my Savior. I've come to see waiting as much more than a reaction to a gap.

Embracing waiting creates a path for flourishing.

5. God Works as I Wait

I've witnessed specific divine intervention through my exploration of waiting on God. It started inside me first. As I've waited on the Lord, I sense a rising level of patience, joy, and gratitude. I'm less focused on what I don't know and more intentional about reflecting on what's true about God. So I'm the same person, but I sense that God's doing something powerful in my soul. I've also been stunned at how God has worked as I've waited on him. By giving God time and resisting my need for quick action, I've seen problems solved, solutions surface, people convicted, and conflict resolved. I've marveled at specific answers to prayer as I've waited. While I knew that God works for those who wait for him, I have firsthand experience that it really happens.

Embracing waiting provides an opportunity for God to work.

Let's Keep Waiting

Life is full of gap moments, opportunities to wait on God. Therefore, I know this book is only the beginning. The issue at hand isn't *if* we wait but *how* we wait. And I hope that you are now better equipped and encouraged to wait. Just to remind you, here's how:

- Honestly: waiting is hard
- Frequently: waiting is common
- Thoughtfully: waiting is biblical
- Patiently: waiting is slow
- Intentionally: waiting is commanded
- Collectively: waiting is relational

There will come a day when our waiting will be over. Our faith will be sight. Everything will be complete. Eternal life will replace our temporary sense of time. It's not that everything will be fast or quick. It's just that there will be no more gaps of vulnerability. What's more, we'll see our God just as he is. We'll know exactly what's true about him because we'll be with him forever.

Until that great day, we're waiting on God.

Rather than waste our waiting with impatience and frustration, we have an opportunity to embrace the surprising comfort of trusting God in the uncertainties of life.

Don't miss the sunrise.
Keep waiting on God.

I believe that I shall look upon the goodness of the LORD
   in the land of the living!
Wait for the LORD;
   be strong, and let your heart take courage;
   wait for the LORD! (Ps. 27:13–14)

Acknowledgments

WRITING A BOOK IS A JOURNEY with dreams, joys, struggles, and sacrifices. And not just for the author, but also for a host of people behind the scenes. Once again, my heart is filled with thankfulness for the grace of God extended to me through family, friends, and ministry colleagues. I'd like to express my profound gratitude.

A small group of readers took time out of their evenings and weekends to read early drafts of the manuscript and offer critiques. Jacki Berg, Kristen Vroegop, Jill Henry, and Dale and Sarah Shaw offered real-world feedback with great suggestions and insightful observations. I'm thankful for the gift of their input. They've made this book much better.

Once again, without the wisdom of Dave DeWit from Crossway and Austin Wilson from Wolgemuth & Wilson, this book wouldn't be a reality. Dave and Austin are both incredibly talented in their areas of expertise, and I'm still stunned that God has allowed my life to be blessed by them.

Over several years of ministry, God provided two bands of brothers who offered encouragement, correction, and comfort to me through countless seasons. The executive pastor team at

College Park walked in real time through countless "gap moments" in ministry. Without pastors Paul Spilker, Bruce Smith, Bill Dinsmore, and Dale Shaw, most of the lessons of this book wouldn't be a reality. And without the Lead Pastor Elder Accountability Team—Stephen Gray, Lance Pfeifer, Micah Vincent, and Eric Edgell—my soul would have been crushed with discouragement. Only Jesus knows how much time, emotion, and wisdom they've given to me. I'm eternally grateful.

My wife, Sarah, joyfully embraces the highs and lows of writing. Her patient listening to my ideas, thoughtful critiques of each chapter, and boundless encouragement when I'm panicked or weary brought this book to life. I'm so thankful that her heart to help people eclipses the challenges associated with supporting a reluctant writer.

Finally, I'm grateful to the people, elders, and staff who call College Park Church home. For over fifteen years it has been my honor to unfold the scriptures Sunday after Sunday as we see how God works for those who wait for him.

I waited and waited and waited for GOD. (Ps. 40:1 MSG)

Appendix 1

The Lord Is . . .

The LORD is a stronghold for the oppressed,
   a stronghold in times of trouble. (Ps. 9:9)

The LORD is king forever and ever;
   the nations perish from his land. (Ps. 10:16)

The LORD is in his holy temple;
   the LORD's throne is in heaven;
   his eyes see, his eyelids test the children of man.
      (Ps. 11:4)

For *the LORD is righteous*;
he loves righteous deeds;
   the upright shall behold his face. (Ps. 11:7)

The LORD is my chosen portion and my cup;
   you hold my lot. (Ps. 16:5)

The LORD *is my rock and my fortress and my deliverer,*
    my God, my rock, in whom I take refuge,
    my shield, and the horn of my salvation, my stronghold.
      (Ps. 18:2)

The LORD *is my shepherd;*
    I shall not want. (Ps. 23:1)

The LORD *is my light and my salvation;*
    whom shall I fear?
The LORD *is the stronghold of my life;*
    of whom shall I be afraid? (Ps. 27:1)

The LORD *is my strength and my shield;*
    in him my heart trusts, and I am helped;
my heart exults,
    and with my song I give thanks to him. (Ps. 28:7)

Oh, taste and see that *the* LORD *is good!*
    Blessed is the man who takes refuge in him! (Ps. 34:8)

The LORD *is merciful and gracious,*
    slow to anger and abounding in steadfast love. (Ps. 103:8)

The LORD *is on my side;* I will not fear.
    What can man do to me? (Ps. 118:6)

The LORD *is my strength and my song;*
    he has become my salvation. (Ps. 118:14)

The LORD is your keeper;
    the LORD is your shade on your right hand. (Ps. 121:5)

The LORD is near to all who call on him,
    to all who call on him in truth. (Ps. 145:18)

Appendix 2

Lord, You Are . . .

But *you, O Lord, are a shield about me,*
  my glory, and the lifter of my head. (Ps. 3:3)

I say to the Lord, "*You are my Lord;*
  I have no good apart from you." (Ps. 16:2)

But I trust in you, O Lord;
  I say, "*You are my God.*" (Ps. 31:14)

You are a hiding place for me;
  you preserve me from trouble;
  you surround me with shouts of deliverance. (Ps. 32:7)

As for me, I am poor and needy,
  but the Lord takes thought for me.
You are my help and my deliverer;
  do not delay, O my God! (Ps. 40:17)

For *you, O Lord, are my hope,*
> my trust, O LORD, from my youth. (Ps. 71:5)

You are the God who works wonders;
> you have made known your might among the peoples.
> > (Ps. 77:14)

For *you, O Lord, are good and forgiving,*
> abounding in steadfast love to all who call upon you. (Ps.
> 86:5)

But *you, O Lord, are a God merciful and gracious,*
> slow to anger and abounding in steadfast love and
> faithfulness. (Ps. 86:15)

You are my God, and I will give thanks to you;
> *you are my God;* I will extol you. (Ps. 118:28)

I cry to you, O LORD;
> I say, "*You are my refuge,*
> my portion in the land of the living." (Ps. 142:5)

Appendix 3

Mapping God's Faithfulness

Instructions

The goal is to trace the faithfulness of God through previous seasons of waiting and rehearse important lessons to fuel endurance. The worksheet has four sections:

- Situation: briefly describe the waiting circumstance
- Resolution: summarize how the situation resolved or concluded
- "God is . . . ": identify a few character qualities of God that were meaningful
- Lesson: record the truth or principle that you learned

Situation	Resolution	"God is"	Lesson

Appendix 4

Waiting in the Psalms

Indeed, none who wait for you shall be put to shame;
   they shall be ashamed who are wantonly treacherous.
      (Ps. 25:3)

Lead me in your truth and teach me,
   for you are the God of my salvation;
   for you I wait all the day long. (Ps. 25:5)

May integrity and uprightness preserve me,
   for I wait for you. (Ps. 25:21)

Wait for the Lord;
   be strong, and let your heart take courage;
   wait for the Lord! (Ps. 27:14)

Be strong, and let your heart take courage,
   all you who wait for the Lord! (Ps. 31:24)

Our soul waits for the LORD;
  he is our help and our shield. (Ps. 33:20)

Be still before the LORD and wait patiently for him;
  fret not yourself over the one who prospers in his way,
  over the man who carries out evil devices! (Ps. 37:7)

For the evildoers shall be cut off,
  but those who wait for the LORD shall inherit the land.
    (Ps. 37:9)

Wait for the LORD and keep his way,
  and he will exalt you to inherit the land;
  you will look on when the wicked are cut off. (Ps. 37:34)

But for you, O LORD, do I wait;
  it is you, O Lord my God, who will answer. (Ps. 38:15)

And now, O Lord, for what do I wait?
  My hope is in you. (Ps. 39:7)

I waited patiently for the LORD;
  he inclined to me and heard my cry. (Ps. 40:1)

I will thank you forever,
  because you have done it.
I will wait for your name, for it is good,
  in the presence of the godly. (Ps. 52:9)

For God alone my soul waits in silence;
   from him comes my salvation. (Ps. 62:1)

For God alone, O my soul, wait in silence,
   for my hope is from him. (Ps. 62:5)

I am weary with my crying out;
   my throat is parched.
My eyes grow dim
   with waiting for my God. (Ps. 69:3)

But they soon forgot his works;
   they did not wait for his counsel. (Ps. 106:13)

I wait for the LORD, my soul waits,
   and in his word I hope. (Ps. 130:5)

My soul waits for the Lord
   more than watchmen for the morning,
   more than watchmen for the morning. (Ps. 130:6)

Bibliography

Brown, Francis, Samuel Driver, and Charles Briggs. *Enhanced Brown-Driver-Briggs Hebrew and English Lexicon*. Oxford, UK: Clarendon Press, 1977.

Dunnam, Maxie. "A Heart Close to God." In *Deepening Your Ministry through Prayer and Personal Growth: 30 Strategies to Transform Your Ministry*, edited by Marshall Shelley. Library of Christian Leadership. Nashville, TN: Moorings, 1996.

Faro, Ingrid Spellnes. "Strength." In *Lexham Theological Wordbook*, edited by Douglas Mangum et al. Lexham Bible Reference Series. Bellingham, WA: Lexham Press, 2014.

Fenlason, Aaron C. "Hope." In *Lexham Theological Wordbook*, edited by Douglas Mangum et al. Lexham Bible Reference Series. Bellingham, WA: Lexham Press, 2014.

Guthrie, Nancy. *Blessed: Experiencing the Promise of the Book of Revelation*. Wheaton, IL: Crossway, 2022.

Hartley, John E. "1994 קָוָה." In *Theological Wordbook of the Old Testament*, edited by R. Laird Harris, Gleason L. Archer Jr., and Bruce K. Waltke. Chicago: Moody, 1999.

Howard, Betsy Childs. *Seasons of Waiting: Walking by Faith When Dreams Are Delayed*. Wheaton, IL: Crossway, 2016.

Lewis, C. S. *Letters to Malcom: Chiefly on Prayer.* San Diego: Harcourt, 1992.

Louw, Johannes P., and Eugene Albert Nida. *Greek-English Lexicon of the New Testament: Based on Semantic Domains.* New York: United Bible Societies, 1996.

Murray, Andrew. *Waiting on God! Daily Messages for a Month.* New York: Revell, 1896.

Patterson, Ben. *Waiting: Finding Hope When God Seems Silent.* Downers Grove, IL: InterVarsity Press, 1989.

Peterson, Eugene. *A Long Obedience in the Same Direction: Discipleship in an Instant Society.* Commemorative Edition. Downers Grove, IL: InterVarsity Press, 2019.

———. *The Message: The Bible in Contemporary Language.* Colorado Springs, CO: NavPress, 2005.

Scazzero, Peter. *The Emotionally Healthy Leader: How Transforming Your Inner Life Will Deeply Transform Your Church, Team, and the World.* Grand Rapids, MI: Zondervan, 2015.

Spurgeon, Charles. *The Promises of God: A New Edition of the Classic Devotional Based on the English Standard Version.* Edited by Tim Chester. Wheaton, IL: Crossway, 2019.

Strong, James. *A Concise Dictionary of the Words in the Greek Testament and the Hebrew Bible.* Bellingham, WA: Logos Bible Software, 2009.

Wald, Chelsea. "Why Your Brain Hates Slowpokes." *Nautilus* (March 2, 2015). Accessed January 21, 2023. https://nautil.us/.

Willard, Dallas. *Renovation of the Heart: Putting on the Character of Christ.* Colorado Springs, CO: NavPress, 2002.

General Index

abiding, 108
Abraham, waiting, 29
ACTS (prayer form), 68
adoration, 50–51, 69
anger, 33–34, 95
anxiety, 34–35, 76, 82, 95
apathy, 35

breathing grace, 79
buying in bulk, 23–24

choosing to wait, 74–77, 80
Christian life, requires waiting,
    xiv–xv, 21, 40, 77
Christlikeness, xiv
church, birthed in waiting, 89–92
collective waiting, 6, 87–101, 110
communication speed, 28
compassion, for those waiting, 96–98
control, desire for, 107
counseling, 95

daily bread, 24
daily waiting, 67–68, 109
dechomai, 44
delayed gratification, xiv
delays, 18
diagnosing when waiting is hard, 21

disappointment, 18–19
discipleship, 40, 81, 95
disdain for waiting, 107
Dunnam, Maxie, 46–47

encouragement, in waiting, 94,
    99–100
eternal life, 110
expectations, 56, 65–66, 71

farming illustration (book of James),
    26, 28
FAST (strategy), 47–54, 56, 68–69
focus, 48–50, 69
forgetfulness, 62
frequency, in waiting, 6, 25–36, 110

gap, between Good Friday and
    Resurrection Sunday, 32
gap-centered mindset, 48
gaps of life, 49, 53, 56, 81, 106, 110
    as redemptive, 106
    as opportunity for faith, 12
God
    faithfulness of, 60–62
    as refuge, 53
    working in our waiting, 109–10
"God is . . . ," 100, 115–17

Scazzero, Peter, 29
seeking, 51–52, 69
social media, 17–18
spiritual empowerment from waiting, 75
spiritual maturity, 109
spiritual watchfulness, 45
Spurgeon, Charles, 38
sunrise, 103–5

tension of waiting, 66–67
thoughtfulness in waiting, 6, 37–54, 106, 110
trust, 43, 52–53, 69

unbelief, 62
uncertainty, 17–18, 39, 62, 63, 74, 81

waiting, 1, 4
    in the Bible, 29–33
    as central to the Christian life, 25–26, 30, 31–32, 36, 81, 96
    as a choice, 74–77, 80
    as a command, 75
    difficulty of, 9–10, 17
    emotional effects of, 28
    as flourishing, 109
    in the Great Commission, 90
    and hoping, 12, 42–43, 51–52, 78
    as identity, 77–80, 82
    and intimacy with God, 109

as invitation to spiritual maturity and godliness, 93
as liberating, 29
looks to the Lord, 13
not culturally easy, 107
not optional for the Christian life, 108
not valued in American culture, 10
as opportunity for spiritual transformation, 80
part of the created order, 27
pushes our limits, 17
requires living by what is true about God, 39
as seeking the Lord, 52
and spiritual maturity, 109
spiritual value of, 10
as vital to Christianity, 6–7
will be over, 110
waiting aware, 68
waiting time, 68, 70
Ward, Chelsea, 28
wasted waiting, 4, 13, 25, 89, 105, 106
watching, 45
watchman, 78–79
weddings, waiting for the bride, 77
Willard, Dallas, 79

yahal, 42
young people, impatience of, 67

Scripture Index

Also Available from Mark Vroegop

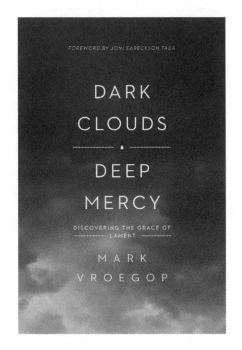

Dark Clouds, Deep Mercy seeks to restore the lost art of lament in order to help readers discover the power of honest wrestling with the questions that come with grief and suffering.

For more information, visit **crossway.org**.

Pro RESTful APIs with Micronaut

Build Java-Based Microservices with REST, JSON, and XML

Second Edition

Sanjay Patni

Apress®

Pro RESTful APIs with Micronaut: Build Java-Based Microservices with REST, JSON, and XML

Sanjay Patni
Santa Clara, CA, USA

ISBN-13 (pbk): 978-1-4842-9199-3   ISBN-13 (electronic): 978-1-4842-9200-6
https://doi.org/10.1007/978-1-4842-9200-6

Managing Director, Apress Media LLC: Welmoed Spahr
Acquisitions Editor: Susan McDermott
Development Editor: Laura Berendson
Coordinating Editor: Jessica Vakili

Distributed to the book trade worldwide by Springer Science+Business Media New York, 233 Spring Street, 6th Floor, New York, NY 10013. Phone 1-800-SPRINGER, fax (201) 348-4505, e-mail orders-ny@springer-sbm.com, or visit www.springeronline.com. Apress Media, LLC is a California LLC and the sole member (owner) is Springer Science + Business Media Finance Inc (SSBM Finance Inc). SSBM Finance Inc is a **Delaware** corporation.

For information on translations, please e-mail booktranslations@springernature.com; for reprint, paperback, or audio rights, please e-mail bookpermissions@springernature.com.

Apress titles may be purchased in bulk for academic, corporate, or promotional use. eBook versions and licenses are also available for most titles. For more information, reference our Print and eBook Bulk Sales web page at http://www.apress.com/bulk-sales.

Any source code or other supplementary material referenced by the author in this book is available to readers on the Github repository: https://github.com/Apress/*Pro-RESTful-APIs-with-Micronaut*. For more detailed information, please visit http://www.apress.com/source-code.

Printed on acid-free paper

I would like to thank everyone at Apress who I've worked closely with. Thanks to the reviewers; their in-depth reviews helped the quality of the book. A heartfelt thanks goes to my wife, Veena, for her tireless and unconditional support that helped me work on this book. A huge thanks goes to my father, Ajit Kumar Patni, and my mother, Late Basantidevi, for their selfless support that helped me reach where I am today.

Table of Contents

About the Author

Sanjay Patni is a results-focused technologist with extensive experience in aligning innovative technology solutions with business needs to optimize manual steps in the business processes and improving operational efficiency.

At Oracle, he has worked with the Fusion Apps Product development team, where he has identified opportunities for automation of programs related to Fusion Apps codeline management. This involved delivery of GA releases for patching, as well as codelines for ongoing demo, development, and testing. He conceptualized and developed self-service UX for codeline requests and auditing, reducing manual steps by 80%. He also rolled out 12 sprints of codeline creation, automating about 100+ manual steps involving integration with other subsystems using technologies like automation workflow and RESTful APIs.

Prior to joining Oracle, he spent 15+ years in the software industry, defining and delivering key initiatives across different industry sectors. His responsibilities included innovation, requirement, analysis, technical architecture, design, and agile software development of web-based enterprise products and solutions. He pioneered innovative usage of Java in building business applications and received an award from Sun Microsystems. This helped improve feedback for Java APIs for Enterprise in building business application software using Java. He has diverse experience in Application Architecture to include UX, Distributed Systems, Cloud and DevOps.

ABOUT THE AUTHOR

He has worked as a visiting technical instructor or mentor and conducted classes or training on RESTful APIs design and integration.

He has a strong educational background in computer science with a master's from IIT, Roorkee, India.

About the Technical Reviewer

Massimo Nardone has more than 22 years of experience in security, web and mobile development, cloud, and IT architecture. His true IT passions are security and Android.

He has been programming and teaching how to program with Android, Perl, PHP, Java, VB, Python, C/C++, and MySQL for more than 20 years.

He holds a master of science degree in computing science from the University of Salerno, Italy.

He has worked as a project manager, software engineer, research engineer, chief security architect, information security manager, PCI/SCADA auditor, and senior lead IT security/cloud/SCADA architect for many years.

His technical skills include security, Android, cloud, Java, MySQL, Drupal, Cobol, Perl, web and mobile development, MongoDB, D3, Joomla, Couchbase, C/C++, WebGL, Python, Pro Rails, Django CMS, Jekyll, Scratch, etc.

He currently works as Chief Information Security Officer (CISO) for Cargotec Oyj.

He worked as visiting lecturer and supervisor for exercises at the Networking Laboratory of the Helsinki University of Technology (Aalto University). He holds four international patents (PKI, SIP, SAML, and Proxy areas).

Massimo has reviewed more than 40 IT books for different publishing companies, and he is the coauthor of *Pro Android Games* (Apress, 2015).

Introduction

Databases, websites, and business applications need to exchange data. This is accomplished by defining standard data formats such as Extensible Markup Language (XML) or JavaScript Object Notation (JSON), as well as transfer protocols or web services such as the Simple Object Access Protocol (SOAP) or the more popular Representational State Transfer (REST). Developers often have to design their own Application Programming Interfaces (APIs) to make applications work while integrating specific business logic around operating systems or servers. This book introduces these concepts with a focus on the RESTful APIs.

This book introduces the data exchange mechanism and common data formats. For web exchange, you will learn the HTTP protocol, including how to use XML. This book compares SOAP and REST and then covers the concepts of stateless transfer. It introduces software API design and best design practices. The second half of the book focuses on RESTful APIs design and implementations that follow the Micronaut and Java API for RESTful Web Services. You will learn how to build and consume Micronaut services using JSON and XML and integrate RESTful APIs with different data sources like relational databases and NoSQL databases through hands-on exercises. You will apply these best practices to complete a design review of publicly available APIs with a small-scale software system in order to design and implement RESTful APIs.

This book is intended for software developers who use data in projects. It is also useful for data professionals who need to understand the methods of data exchange and how to interact with business applications. Java programming experience is required for the exercises.

INTRODUCTION

Topics include

- Data exchange and web services
- SOAP vs. REST, state vs. stateless
- XML vs. JSON
- Introduction to API design: REST and Micronaut
- API design practices
- Designing RESTful APIs
- Building RESTful APIs
- Interacting with RDBMS (MySQL)
- Consuming RESTful APIs (i.e., JSON, XML)

CHAPTER 1

Fundamentals of RESTful APIs

Abstract

APIs are not new. They've served as interfaces that enable applications to communicate with each other for decades. But the role of APIs has changed dramatically in the last few years. Innovative companies have discovered that APIs can be used as an interface to the business, allowing them to monetize digital assets, extend their value proposition with partner-delivered capabilities, and connect to customers across channels and devices. When you create an API, you are allowing others within or outside of your organization to make use of your service or product to create new applications, attract customers, or expand their business. Internal APIs enhance the productivity of development teams by maximizing reusability and enforcing consistency in new applications. Public APIs can add value to your business by allowing third-party developers to enhance your services or bring their customers to you. As developers find new applications for your services and data, a network effect occurs, delivering significant bottom-line business impact. For example, Expedia opened up their travel booking services to partners through an API to launch the Expedia Affiliate Network, building a new revenue stream that now contributes $2B in annual revenue. Salesforce released APIs to enable partners to extend the capabilities of their platform and now generates half of their annual revenue through those APIs, which could be SOAP based (JAX-WS) and, more recently, RESTful (JAX-RS), Spring Boot, and now Micronaut.

A SOAP web service depends upon a number of technologies (such as UDDI, WSDL, SOAP, HTTP) and protocols to transport and transform data between a service provider and the consumer and can be created with JAX-WS.

Later, Roy Fielding (in the year 2000) presented his doctoral dissertation, "Architectural Styles and the Design of Network-based Software Architecture." He coined the term "REST," an architectural style for distributed hypermedia systems. Put simply, REST (short for REpresentational State Transfer) is an architectural style defined to help create and organize distributed systems. The keyword from that definition should be "style," because an important aspect of REST (and which is one of the main reasons books like this one exist) is that it is an architectural style—not a guideline, not a standard, or anything that would imply that there are a set of hard rules to follow in order to end up having a RESTful architecture.

In this chapter, I'll be covering REST fundamentals, SOAP vs. REST, and web architectural style to provide a solid foundation and better prepare you for what you'll see in later chapters.

The main idea behind REST is that a distributed system, organized RESTfully, will improve in the following areas:

- Performance: The communication style proposed by REST is meant to be efficient and simple, allowing a performance boost on systems that adopt it.

- Scalability of component interaction: Any distributed system should be able to handle this aspect well enough, and the simple interaction proposed by REST greatly allows for this.

- Simplicity of interface: A simple interface allows for simpler interactions between systems, which in turn can grant benefits like the ones previously mentioned.

- Modifiability of components: The distributed nature of the system, and the separation of concerns proposed by REST (more on this in a bit), allows for components to be modified independently of each other at a minimum cost and risk.

- Portability: REST is technology and language agnostic, meaning that it can be implemented and consumed by any type of technology (there are some constraints that I'll go over in a bit, but no specific technology is enforced).

- Reliability: The stateless constraint proposed by REST (more on this later) allows for the easier recovery of a system after failure.

- Visibility: Again, the stateless constraint proposed has the added full state of said request (this will become clear once I talk about the constraints in a bit). From this list, some direct benefits can be extrapolated. A component-centric design allows you to make systems that are very fault tolerant. Having the failure of one component not affect the entire stability of the system is a great benefit for any system. Interconnecting components is quite easy, minimizing the risks when adding new features or scaling up or down. A system designed with REST in mind will be accessible to a wider audience, thanks to its portability (as described earlier). With a generic interface, the system can be used by a wider range of developers. In order to achieve these properties and benefits, a set of constraints were added to REST to help define a uniform connector interface. REST is not suggested to use when you need to enforce a strict contract between a client and a server and when performing transactions that involve multiple calls.

SOAP vs. REST

Table 1-1 has a comparison between SOAP and REST with an example of use cases each can support.

Table 1-1. SOAP vs. REST comparison

Topic	SOAP	REST
Origin	SOAP (Simple Object Access Protocol) was created in 1998 by Dave Winer et al. in collaboration with Microsoft. Developed by a large software company, this protocol addresses the goal of addressing the needs of the enterprise market	REST (Representational State Transfer) was created in 2000 by Roy Fielding at UC, Irvine. Developed in an academic environment, this protocol embraces the philosophy of the open Web
Basic Concept	Makes data available as services (verb + noun), for example, "getUser" or "PayInvoice"	Makes data available as resources (nouns), for example, "user" or "invoice"
Pros	Follows a formal enterprise approach Works on top of any communication protocol, even asynchronously Information about objects is communicated to clients Security and authorization are part of the protocol Can be fully described using WSDL	Follows the philosophy of the open Web Relatively easy to implement and maintain Clearly separates client and server implementations Communication isn't controlled by a single entity Information can be stored by the client to prevent multiple calls Can return data in multiple formats (JSON, XML, etc.)
Cons	Spends a lot of bandwidth communicating metadata Hard to implement and is unpopular among web and mobile developers	Only works on top of the HTTP protocol Hard to enforce authorization and security on top of it

(continued)

Table 1-1. (*continued*)

Topic	SOAP	REST
When to use	When clients need to have access to objects available on servers When you want to enforce a formal contract between a client and a server	When clients and servers operate on a web environment When information about objects doesn't need to be communicated to the client
When not to use	When you want the majority of developers to easily use your API When your bandwidth is very limited	When you need to enforce a strict contract between a client and a server When performing transactions that involve multiple calls
Use cases	Financial services Payment gateways Telecommunication services	Social media services Social networks Web chat services Mobile services
Examples	`www.salesforce.com/developer/docs/api/`— Salesforce SOAP API	`https://dev.twitter.com/`
Conclusion	Use SOAP if you are dealing with transactional operations and you already have an audience that is satisfied with this technology	Use REST if you're focused on wide-scale API adoption or if your API is targeted at mobile apps

Web Architectural Style

According to Fielding, there are two ways to define a system:

- One is to start from a blank slate—an empty whiteboard—with no initial knowledge of the system being built or the use of familiar components until the needs are satisfied.

- A second approach is to start with the full set of needs for the system, and constraints are added to individual components until the forces that influence the system are able to interact in harmony with each other.

REST follows the second approach. In order to define a REST architecture, a null state is initially defined—a system that has no constraints whatsoever and where component differentiation is nothing but a myth—and constraints are added one by one. The following subsections cover web architectural style constraints. Each of these constraints defines how the framework for RESTful APIs should be architected and designed. Security is another aspect which needs to be considered independently as part of this framework when rolling out RESTful APIs to the end users.

Client-Server

The separation of concerns is the core theme of the Web's client-server constraints.

The Web is a client-server-based system, in which clients and servers have distinct parts to play.

They may be implemented and deployed independently, using any language or technology, so long as they conform to the Web's uniform interface.

Uniform Resource Interface

The interactions between the Web's components—meaning its clients, servers, and network-based intermediaries—depend on the uniformity of their interfaces.

Web components interoperate consistently within the uniform interface's four constraints, which Fielding identified as

- Identification of resources

- Manipulation of resources through representations

- Self-descriptive messages

- Hypermedia as the engine of application state (HATEOAS)

Layered System

Generally speaking, a network-based intermediary will intercept client-server communication for a specific purpose.

Network-based intermediaries are commonly used for enforcement of security, response caching, and load balancing.

The layered system constraints enable network-based intermediaries such as proxies and gateways to be transparently deployed between a client and a server using the Web's uniform interface.

Caching

Caching is one of web architecture's most important constraints. The cache constraints instruct a web server to declare the cache ability of each response's data.

Caching response data can help to reduce client-perceived latency, increase the overall availability and reliability of an application, and control a web server's load. In a word, caching reduces the overall cost of the Web.

Stateless

The stateless constraint dictates that a web server is not required to memorize the state of its client applications. As a result, each client must include all of the contextual information that it considers relevant in each interaction with the web server.

Web servers ask clients to manage the complexity of communicating their application state so that the web server can service a much larger number of clients. This trade-off is a key contributor to the scalability of the Web's architectural style.

Code on Demand

The Web makes heavy use of code on demand, a constraint which enables web servers to temporarily transfer executable programs, such as scripts or plug-ins, to clients.

Code on demand tends to establish a technology coupling between web servers and their clients, since the client must be able to understand and execute the code that it downloads on demand from the server. For this reason, code on demand is the only constraint of the Web's architectural style that is considered optional.

HATEOAS

The final principle of REST is the idea of using hypermedia as the engine of application state (HATEOAS). When developing a client-server solution using HATEOAS, the logic on the server side might change independently of the clients.

Hypermedia is a document-centric approach with the added support for embedding links to other services and information within the document format.

One of the uses of hypermedia and hyperlinks is composing complex sets of information from disparate sources. The information could be within a company private cloud or within a public cloud from disparate sources.

Example:

```
<podcast id="111">
  <customer>http://customers.myintranet.com/customers/1</
customers>
  <link>http://podcast.com/myfirstpodcast</link>
  <description> This is my first podcast </description>
</podcast>
```

Each of these web architecture styles adds beneficial properties to the web system.

By adopting these constraints, teams can build simple, visible, usable, accessible, evolvable, flexible, maintainable, reliable, scalable, and performant systems as shown in Table 1-2.

Table 1-2. *Constraint and system property*

By Following the Constraint	Gain the Following System Property
Client-server interactions	Simple, evolvable, scalable
Stateless communications	Simple, visible, maintainable, evolvable, and reliable
Cacheable data	Visible, scalable, and performant
Uniform interfaces	Simple, usable, visible, accessible, evolvable, and reliable
Layered system	Flexible, scalable, reliable, and performant
Code on demand	Evolvable

Note   I have not covered security in this book as part of REST fundamentals, but security is very important for rolling out RESTful APIs.

What Is REST?

We have briefly introduced REST with REST API fundamentals in the previous section. This section has further introductory details about REST concepts.

"REST" was coined by Roy Fielding in his Ph.D. dissertation to describe a design pattern for implementing networked systems. REST is Representational State Transfer, an architectural style for designing distributed systems. It's not a standard, but rather a set of constraints. It's not tied to HTTP, but is associated most commonly with it.

REST Basics

Unlike SOAP and XML-RPC, REST does not really require a new message format. The HTTP API is CRUD (Create, Retrieve, Update, and Delete):

- GET = "give me some info" (Retrieve)

- POST = "here's some update info" (Update)

- PUT = "here's some new info" (Create)

- DELETE = "delete some info" (Delete)

- And more....

- PATCH = The HTTP method PATCH can be used to update partial resources. For instance, when you only need to update one field of the resource, PUTting a complete resource representation might be cumbersome and utilizes more bandwidth.

- HEAD = The **HEAD** method is identical to the GET method, except that the server must not return a message body in the response. This method is often used for testing hypertext links for validity, accessibility, and recent modification.

- OPTIONS = This method allows the client to determine the options and/or requirements associated with a resource or the capabilities of a server, without implying a resource action or initiating a resource retrieval.

- Notion of "idempotency": The idea that when sending a GET, DELETE, or PUT to the system, the effect should be the same whether the command is sent one or more times, but POST creates an entity in the collection and therefore is not idempotent.

REST Fundamentals

Just to remind you, about 8356 APIs were written in REST by ProgrammableWeb.com in 2016. REST is a resource-based architecture. A resource is accessed via a common interface based on the HTTP standard methods. REST asks developers to use HTTP methods explicitly and in a way that's consistent with the protocol definition. Each resource is identified by a URL. Every resource should support the HTTP common operations, and REST allows that resource to have different representations, for example, text, xml, json, etc. The REST client can ask for a specific representation via the HTTP protocol (content negotiation). Table 1-3 describes data elements used in REST.

Table 1-3. *Structures of REST*

Data Element	Description
Resource	Conceptual target of a hypertext reference, e.g., customer/order
Resource Identifier	A uniform resource locator (URL) or uniform resource name (URN) identifying a specific resource, e.g., `http://myrest.com/customer/3435`
Resource Metadata	Information describing the resource, e.g., tag, author, source link, alternate location, alias names
Representation	The resource content—JSON Message, HTML Document, JPEG Image
Representation Metadata	Information describing how to process the representation, e.g., media type, last-modified time
Control Data	Information describing how to optimize response processing, e.g., if-modified-since, cache-control-expiry

Let's look at some examples.

Resources

First, here's a REST resource to GET a list of podcasts:

```
http://prorest/podcasts
```

Next, here's a REST resource to GET details of podcast id 1:

```
http://prorest/podcasts/1
```

Representations

Here is an XML representation of a response—GET customer for an id:

```
<Customer>
  <id>123</id>
  <name>John</name>
</Customer>
```

Next, here's a JSON representation of a response—GET customer for an id:

```
{"Customer":{"id":"123","name":"John"}}
```

Content Negotiation

HTTP natively supports a mechanism based on headers to tell the server about the content you expect and you're able to handle. Based on these hints, the server is responsible for returning the corresponding content in the correct format. Figure 1-1 shows an example.

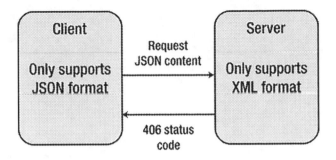

Figure 1-1. *Content negotiation*

If the server doesn't support the requested format, it will send back a 406 status code (Not Acceptable) to notify the client that made the request ("The requested resource is only capable of generating content not acceptable according to the Accept headers sent in the request") according to the specification.

Summary

REST identifies the key architectural principles of why the Web is prevalent and scalable. The next step in the education of the Web is to apply these principles to the semantics Web and the world of web services. REST offers a simple, interoperable, and flexible way of writing web services that can be very different than the WS-* that so many of you had training in. In the next chapter, we will introduce Micronaut—A morder JVM based, full-stack framework for building modular, easily testable micro service and server less applications. We will also compare it with similar framework Spring Boot.

CHAPTER 2

Micronaut

Abstract

Micronaut is a JVM-based modern full-stack microservice framework. This new framework has been developed by the Grails team with an intention to solve problems which have been identified over the years while building the real-world microservices applications.

One of the most exciting features of Micronaut is its compile-time dependency injection mechanism. Most frameworks use reflection and proxies to perform dependency injection at runtime. Micronaut, however, builds its dependency injection data at compile time. The result is faster application startup and smaller memory footprints.

I think it is not an exaggeration if I say we are living in the age of microservices. Microservices became the de facto architecture pattern for every new enterprise-scale application that is being implemented, and many existing monolithic applications are getting migrated into microservices. In the case of the Java world, Spring Boot turned out to be the standard framework to develop microservices. There were some other frameworks like DropWizard, Apache Karaf, and Jersey. But they were not able to give tough competition to Spring Boot, and slowly their usage percentage came down and became insignificant over a period of time. If you observe the evolution of Spring Boot, initially it was not proposed as a microservices solution from Spring. It was initially proposed and implemented as the containerless web application, and the developer community started using it for microservices implementation. But Spring Boot got its own limitations like

- Fixed single language

- Lack of built-in support for data accessing

- Lack of simpler unit testing

- Lack of built-in service discovery

- Lack of built-in load balancing

We need explicit configuration which can be achieved through the cloud services instead of having the built-in support within the framework itself.

Here comes Micronaut which contains the aforementioned built-in features and designed with single and primary intent to serve as the vehicle for microservices development.

Comparison of Micronaut with Spring Boot
Ease of Installation

Both Spring Boot and Micronaut won't be complex for installation and can be installed easily by following the installation instructions. Both frameworks need the following prerequisites:

- A favorite text editor or IDE

- JDK 1.8 or later

- Gradle or Maven latest versions

The code which has been generated through the CLI tool can be directly imported into your IDE:

- Spring Tool Suite (STS): Spring Boot

- Visual Studio Code: Micronaut

Natively Cloud Enabled

When it comes to Spring Boot, to support the previously discussed cloud-specific features, we need to depend on the third-party cloud services or libraries; it doesn't support any of the above-listed features by default, so Micronaut has an advantage here.

The following list of cloud-specific features is directly integrated into the Micronaut runtime:

- Service discovery.

- Eureka, Consul, or ZooKeeper service discovery servers are being supported.

- The Kubernetes container runtime is supported by default.

- Client-side load balancing.

- Netflix Ribbon can be used for load balancing.

- Distributed configuration.

- Distributed tracing.

- Serverless functions.

Serverless Functions

Serverless architecture, where developers will deploy the function. From there onward, they are completely managed by the cloud environment, that is, invocation, execution, and control. But Micronaut's fast startup time, compile-time approach, and low-memory footprint make this framework a great candidate for developing functions, and in fact, Micronaut features have the dedicated support for implementing and deploying functions to the AWS Lambda and any FaaS system that supports running functions as containers.

Application Configuration

Micronaut inspired from both Grails and Spring Boot in integrating configuration properties from different sources directly into the core IoC container. Configurations can be provided by default in either YAML, JSON, Java properties, or Groovy files. The convention is to search for a file called application.yml, application.properties, application.json, or application.groovy.

- Command-line arguments

- Properties from SPRING_APPLICATION_JSON (only if there is any Spring dependency)

- Properties from MICRONAUT_APPLICATION_JSON

- Java system properties

- OS environment variables

- Each environment-specific properties like application-{environment}.{extension} (could be .properties, .json, .yml, or .groovy)

- Application-specific properties from the application.{extension} (could be .properties, .json, .yml, or .groovy)

- Special properties (random values)

Spring Boot supports all the preceding property locations; in addition, it also supports other property locations:

- Spring Boot devtools global settings properties

- @TestPropertySource annotations on your tests

- @SpringBootTest#properties annotation attribute on your tests

- ServletConfig init parameters

- ServletContext init parameters

- JNDI attributes from java:comp/env

- @PropertySource annotations on your @Configuration classes

- Default properties (specified by setting SpringApplication.setDefaultProperties)

"Spring Boot provided more ways to handle with properties when we compared it against Micronaut."

Messaging System Support

Spring Boot supports the integration of external messaging systems, such as

- RabbitMQ

- Apache Kafka

- ActiveMQ

- Artemis

Micronaut also supports the popular messaging systems, such as

- RabbitMQ

- Apache Kafka

"Micronaut has the embedded support for the Apache Kafka." "Both frameworks have the support of the popular messaging systems but Spring Boot supports more tools."

Security

Spring Boot supports the following security mechanisms by default:

- MVC Security

- WebFlux Security

- OAuth2

- Actuator Security

Micronaut supports the following security mechanisms by default:

- Authentication Providers

- Security Rules

- IP Pattern Rule

- Secured Annotation

- Intercept URL Map

- Built-In Endpoints Security

- Authentication Strategies

- Basic Auth

- Session Authentication

- JSON Web Token

- Built-In Security Controllers

- Retrieve the Authenticated User

- Security Events

Caching

Spring Boot supports the following caching providers:

- Redis

- Couchbase

- Generic

- JCache (JSR-107)

- EhCache 2.x

- Hazelcast

- Infinispan

- Caffeine

Micronaut supports the following list of caching providers:

- Caffeine (by default, Micronaut supports it)

- Redis

"Obviously, Spring Boot is leading in supporting caching providers."

Management and Monitoring

Micronaut inspired by the Grails, Spring Boot, and Micronaut management dependency adds support to monitor your applications via endpoints, the special URIs that return details about the state of your application and health:

- Creating endpoints

- Built-in endpoints

API Portfolio

This book will take three business domain problems and build a portfolio of APIs.

Online Flight

To illustrate features of Micronaut, this book will take an example of an "online flight" application. The application will enable passengers to view flight they are traveling. You will define two component classes:

1. A service component that lets a passenger see what flights they are booked in.

2. A repository component that stores passengers for a flight. Initially, you will store passengers in memory for simplicity.

Object	Field	Type
Passenger	Name	String
Flight	Origin	String
	Destination	String
	Departure	Datetime
	Flight#	int

Message

This API will enable sending messages to the users in the system.

Object	Fields	Type
Message	Message	String
	From	String
	To	String
	Creation Date	Date

Quote

To illustrate features of Micronaut data, this book will take an example of an "online quote" application. The application will enable buyers to create and view quotes including products they want to buy. You will define three component classes:

1. Catalog to list products with their price

2. Quote for a customer including line items of the products with total price

3. Quote line item including products with unit price and quantity

Object	Field	Type
Product	Name	String
	Description	String
	Unit Price	Float
Quote	Customer	String
	Quote Date	Date
	Address	Object

Object	Field	Type
	Quote Line	Object
	Total Price	Float
Quote Line	Product	Object
	Quantity	Long
	Unit Price	Float

Software

This book will use the following software for the coding problems.

Micronaut

https://micronaut.io/download/

INSTALLING WITH SDKMAN!

This tool makes installing the Micronaut framework on any Unix-based platform (Mac OSX, Linux, Cygwin, Solaris, or FreeBSD) easy.

Simply open a new terminal and enter

```
$ curl -s https://get.sdkman.io | bash
```

Follow the on-screen instructions to complete installation. Open a new terminal or type the command:

```
$ source "$HOME/.sdkman/bin/sdkman-init.sh"
```

Then install the latest stable version of the framework:

```
$ sdk install micronaut
```

If prompted, make this your default version.

After installation is complete, it can be tested with

```
$ mn --version
```

That's all there is to it!
Now let's create "hello from Micronaut."
It is assumed that micronaut 3, gradle and jdk11 is installed.
mn create-app hello-world

JDK 11

```
https://jdk.java.net/archive/
```

POSTMAN

```
www.postman.com/downloads/
```

CURL

```
https://curl.se/download.html
```

IDE

You have two choices to use the IDE.

Visual Studio Code

```
https://code.visualstudio.com/download
```

IntelliJ

```
www.jetbrains.com/idea/download/
```

Maven

```
https://maven.apache.org/download.cgi
```

Setting Up an IDE

The application created in the previous section contains a "main class" located in src/main/java that looks like the following:

```
package hello.world;
import io.micronaut.runtime.Micronaut;
public class Application {
    public static void main(String[] args) {
        Micronaut.run(Application.class);
    }
}
```

This is the class that is run when running the application via Gradle or via deployment.

Configuring Visual Studio Code

In this book, we will illustrate the use of Visual Studio Code for editing Java code.

Open code created in the hello-world folder by clicking "Open" and navigating to the hello-world folder. Micronaut can be set up within Visual Studio Code. You will need to first install the Java Extension Pack.

6. Visual Studio IntelliCode

Install the Extension Pack for Java

To get started with this extension pack,

Extension Pack for Java is a collection of popular extensions that can help write, test, and debug Java applications in Visual Studio Code. Visual Studio Code support currently only works for Maven builds. The hello world example will run using the command line since it uses gradle.

https://code.visualstudio.com/docs/java/extensions

Once the extension pack is installed, you could use an IDE for editing Java code.

Now create a new class using File ➤ New File ➤ New Java Class and paste

```
package hello.world;
import io.micronaut.http.MediaType;
import io.micronaut.http.annotation.Controller;
import io.micronaut.http.annotation.Get;
@Controller("/hello") public class HelloController {
@Get(produces = MediaType.TEXT_PLAIN)
public String index() {return "Hello from Micronaut"; }
 }
```

Save the file as HelloController.java. Files will look like the preceding example. Now to run from the command prompt

```
cd ~/hello-world
./gradlew run
curl http://localhost:8080/hello
```

You can also run the application from an IDE by selecting Application. java and right-clicking and running.

```
https://walkingtreetech.medium.com/spring-boot-vs-micronaut-
the-battle-unleashed-2682354a88e9
```

Summary

In this chapter, we reviewed features of Micronaut and compared those with Spring Boot. We also analyzed sample domains—flight status message, and quote to create a portfolio of APIs using Micronaut.

CHAPTER 3

Introduction: XML and JSON

Abstract

This chapter introduces basic concepts about XML and JSON. At the end of this chapter, there is an exercise to demonstrate XML and JSON responses from a Micronaut app.

What Is XML?

eXtensible Markup Language (XML) is a text-based markup language which is a standard for data interchange on the Web. As with HTML, you identify data using tags (identifiers enclosed in angle brackets, like this: <...>). Collectively, the tags are known as "markup." It puts a label on a piece of data that identifies it (e.g., <message>...</message>). In the same way that you define the field names for a data structure, you are free to use any XML tags that make sense for a given application. Naturally, though, for multiple applications to use the same XML data, they have to agree on the tag names they intend to use. Here is an example of some XML data you might use for a messaging application:

```
<message>
<to>you@yourAddress.com</to>
<from>me@myAddress.com</from>
<subject>XML Is Really Cool>
</subject>
<text>
How many ways is XML cool? Let me count the ways...
</text>
</message>
```

Tags can also contain attributes (additional information included as part of the tag itself) within the tag's angle brackets. If you consider the information in question to be part of the essential material that is being expressed or communicated in the XML, put it in an element. For human-readable documents, this generally means the core content that is being communicated to the reader. For machine-oriented record formats, this generally means the data that comes directly from the problem domain. If you consider the information to be peripheral or incidental to the main communication, or purely intended to help applications process the main communication, use attributes. The following example shows an email message structure that uses attributes for the to, from, and subject fields:

```
<message to=you@yourAddress.com from=me@myAddress.com
subject="XML Is Really Cool">
<text>
How many ways is XML cool? Let me count the ways...
</text>
</message>
```

One really big difference between XML and HTML is that an XML document is always constrained to be well formed. There are several rules that determine when a document is well formed, but one of the most important is that every tag has a closing tag. So, in XML, the `</to>` tag is not optional. The `<to>` element is never terminated by any tag other than `</to>`.

Note   Another important aspect of a well-formed document is that all tags are completely nested. So you can have `<message>..<to>..</to>..</message>`, but never `<message>..<to>..</message>..</to>`.

An XML Schema is a language for expressing constraints about XML documents. There are several different schema languages in widespread use, but the main ones are Document Type Definitions (DTDs). It defines the legal building blocks of an XML document. It also defines the document structure with a list of legal elements and attributes.

XML Comments

XML comments look just like HTML comments:

```
<message to=you@yourAddress.com from=me@myAddress.com
subject="XML Is Really Cool">
<!-- This is comment -->
<text>
How many ways is XML cool? Let me count the ways...
</text>
</message>
```

To complete this introduction to XML, note that an XML file always starts with a prolog. The minimal prolog contains a declaration that identifies the document as an XML document, like this:

```
<?xml version="1.0"?>
```

The declaration may also contain additional information, like this:

```
<?xml version="1.0" encoding="ISO-8859-1" standalone="yes"?>
```

- version: Identifies the version of the XML markup language used in the data. This attribute is not optional.

- encoding: Identifies the character set used to encode the data. "ISO-8859-1" is "Latin-1," the Western European and English language character set. (The default is compressed Unicode: UTF-8.)

- standalone: Tells whether or not this document references an external entity or an external data type specification. If there are no external references, then "yes" is appropriate.

Why Is XML Important?

It is important because it allows the flexible development of user-defined document types, which means that it provides a persistent, robust, nonproprietary, and verifiable file format which can be used for the storage and transmission of data for both on and off the Web. In addition, XML

- Provides plain text: Plain text makes it readable.

- Provides data identification: By use of tags, data can be identified.

- Provides styleability: Using XSLT (Extensible Stylesheet Language Transformations), data can be made in a presentable form.

- Is easily processed (XML parsers, as well as well-formed parsers).

- Is hierarchical (through nested tags).

How Can You Use XML?

There are several basic ways to make use of XML:

- Document driven programming, where XML documents are containers that build interfaces and applications from existing components

- Archiving: The foundation for document-driven programming, where the customized version of a component is saved (archived) so it can be used later

- Binding, where the DTD or schema that defines an XML data structure is used to automatically generate a significant portion of the application that will eventually process that data

Pros and Cons of XML

Some of the pros and cons of XML are explained as follows:

- Pros

  - Readable and editable by developers.

  - Error checking by means of schema and DTDs.

  - Can represent complex hierarchies of data.

  - Unicode gives flexibility for international operation.

  - Plenty of tools in all computer languages for both creation and parsing.

- Cons

  - Bulky text with low payload/formatting ratio (but can be compressed).

- Both creation and client-side parsing are CPU intensive.

- Common word processing characters are illegal (MS Word "smart" punctuation, for example).

- Images and other binary data require extra encoding.

What Is JSON?

JSON or JavaScript Object Notation is a lightweight text-based open standard designed for human-readable data interchange. Conventions used by JSON are known to programmers, which include those with knowledge of C, C++, Java, Python, Perl, etc.

- The format was specified by Douglas Crockford.

- It was designed for human-readable data interchange.

- It has been extended from the JavaScript scripting language.

- The filename extension is `.json`.

- The JSON Internet media type is `application/json`.

- JSON is easy to read and write.

- JSON is language independent.

JSON Syntax

In this section, we will discuss what JSON's basic data types are and their syntax. Figure 3-1 shows the basic data types of JSON.

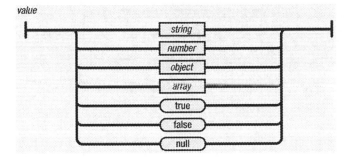

Figure 3-1. *Basic data types*

Strings

Strings are enclosed in double quotes and can contain the usual assortment of escaped characters.

Numbers

Numbers have the usual C/C++/Java syntax, including exponential (E) notation. All numbers are decimal—no octal or hexadecimal.

Objects

An object is an unordered set of a name/value pair. The pairs are enclosed within braces ({ }).

Example:

```
{ "name": "html", "years": 5 }
```

Pairs are separated by commas. There is a colon between the name and the value.

The syntax of a JSON object is shown in Figure 3-2.

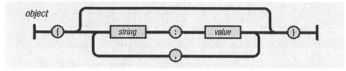

Figure 3-2. *JSON object*

Arrays

An array is an ordered collection of values. The values are enclosed within brackets. The syntax of JSON arrays is shown in Figure 3-3.

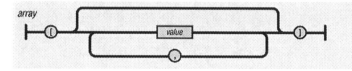

Figure 3-3. *JSON arrays*

Booleans

It can have either true or false values.

Null

The value is that it's empty.

Why Is JSON Important?

There is a reason why JSON is becoming very popular as a data exchange format (more important than it being less verbose than XML): programmers are sick of writing parsers! But "wait," you say. "Surely there are XML parsers available for you to use so that you don't have to roll your own." Yes, there are. But while XML parsers handle the low-level syntactic parsing of XML tags, attributes, etc., you still need to walk the DOM tree or, worse, build one yourself with nothing but a SAX parser (Objective-C iPhone SDK I'm looking at you!). And that code you write will of course depend on whether the XML you need to make sense of looks like this:

```
1 <person first-name="John" last-name="Smith"/>
```

or this:

```
1 <person>
2 <first-name>John</first-name>
3 <last-name>Smith</last-name>
4 </person>
```

or this:

```
1 <object type="Person">
2 <property name="first-name">John</property>
3 <property name="last-name">Smith</property>
4 </object>
```

or any of the myriad of other ways one can conceive of expressing the same concept (and there are many). The standard XML parser does not help you in this regard. You still need to do some work with the parse tree.

Working with JSON is a different, and superior, experience. First, the simpler syntax helps you avoid the need to decide between many different ways of representing your data (as we saw earlier with XML), much less which rope to hang yourself with. Usually, there is only one straightforward way to represent something:

```
1 { "first-name" : "John",
2 "last-name" : "Smith" }
```

How Can You Use JSON?

The following discusses how you can use JSON:

- It is used while writing JavaScript-based applications that include browser extensions and websites.

- JSON format is used for serializing and transmitting structured data over a network connection. It is primarily used to transmit data between a server and web applications.

- Web services and APIs use JSON format to provide public data.

Pros and Cons of JSON

The following are pros and cons of JSON:

Pros

- Easy to read/write/parse

- Reasonably succinct (compared with XML, for instance)

- Common "standard" with many libraries available

Cons

- Not as light as binary formats.

- Can't use comments.

- It's "encapsulated," meaning that you can't readily stream/append data, but have to break it up into individual objects. XML has the same problem, whereas CSV does not.

- Difficult to describe the data you're presenting (easier with XML).

- Unable to enforce, or validate against, a structure/schema.

XML and JSON Comparison

This section compares XML and JSON based upon different properties.

Table 3-1. *XML and JSON comparison*

Property	XML	JSON
Simplicity	XML is simple and human-readable	JSON is much simpler than XML as well as human-readable
Self-Describing	Yes	Yes
Processing	XML is processed easily	JSON is processed more easily because its structure is simpler
Performance	Not optimized for performance due to tags	Faster than XML because of size
Openness	XML is open	JSON is at least as open as XML, perhaps more so because it is not in the center of a corporate/political standardization struggle
Object-Oriented	XML is document oriented	JSON is data oriented. JSON can be mapped more easily to object-oriented systems
Interoperability	XML is interoperable	JSON has the same interoperability potential as XML

(*continued*)

Table 3-1. (*continued*)

Property	XML	JSON
Internationalization	Supports Unicode	Supports Unicode
Extendability	XML is extensible	JSON is not extensible because it does not need to be. JSON is not a document markup language, so it is not necessary to define new tags or attributes to represent data in it
Adoption	XML is widely adopted by the industry	JSON is just beginning to become known. Its simplicity and the ease of converting XML to JSON makes JSON ultimately more adoptable

Implementing APIs to Return XML and JSON Messages

`https://micronaut.io/launch/`

As per the screen, select

Application Type: Micronaut Application

Java Version: 11

Name: message

Package: com.rest

Build Tool: maven

Click "Generate Project."

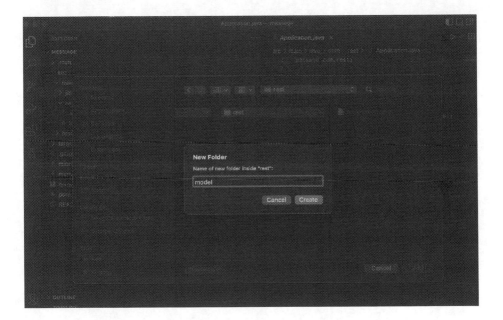

Your Micronaut app is ready for takeoff.

Unix/Linux/macOS   Windows

Unzip the archive

```
unzip message.zip
```

cd into the project

```
cd message
```

Launch!

```
./mvnw mn:run
```

Once you've gotten your new project started, you can continue your journey by reviewing our documentation and learning resources

CLOSE   START OVER

Open message in Visual Source Code.

Now add a new folder model by selecting File ➤ Add new folder and navigating to code generated by Micronaut.

Then create a new domain class Message.

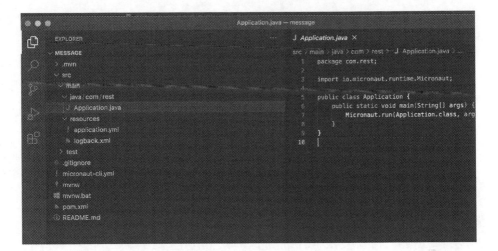

The following code creates a domain object Message with an attribute message. Getter and setter methods are created in the IDE.

```java
package com.rest.model;

import javax.validation.constraints.NotNull;

public class Message {
 @NotNull
 private String message;
 public String getMessage() {
        return message;
 }
 public void setMessage(String message) {
     this.message = message;
 }
}
~
```

Now create a new folder controller after navigating to message code generated by Micronaut.

The following code exposes two endpoints:

a. message/xml for getting the message attribute
    value in XML

b. Message/json for getting the message attribute value
    in JSON format

Create a controller:

```
package com.rest.controllers;
import com.rest.model.Message;
import io.micronaut.http.annotation.Get;
import io.micronaut.http.annotation.Controller;
import io.micronaut.http.HttpResponse;
import io.micronaut.http.MediaType;
import io.micronaut.http.annotation.Produces;

@Controller("/message")  // <2>
public class MessageController {

  @Produces(MediaType.TEXT_XML)
  @Get("/xml")
    public HttpResponse<?> messageXml() {
        Message message = new Message();
        message.setMessage("Hello from Micronaut");
        final String xml = encodeAsXml(message);
        return HttpResponse.ok(xml).contentType(MediaType.
        APPLICATION_XML_TYPE);
    }
  @Produces(MediaType.TEXT_JSON)
  @Get("/json")
    public HttpResponse<?> messageJson() {
        Message message = new Message();
        message.setMessage("Hello from Micronaut");
```

```java
    return HttpResponse.ok(message);
}

private String encodeAsXml(final Message message) {
    return String.format("<message>%s</message>", message.
    getMessage());
}

}
```

You should have files as shown earlier.

Run the app in the IDE using Run ➤ Run without Debugging.

You could also run in the IDE by selecting Application.java and then right-clicking it.

Using POSTMAN as per the screenshot view JSON and XML response of message

Summary

In this chapter, we reviewed messaging using XML and JSON formats and compared them. Then we developed APIs to return XML and JSON responses from a Micronaut app.

CHAPTER 4

API Design and Modeling

Abstract

This chapter starts with API design strategies and then goes into API creation process and modeling. Best practices for REST API design are discussed, followed by API solution architecture. In the exercises, a simple API is designed for podcast subscription and then modeling using OpenAPI.

API Design Strategies

As the UI is to UX (user experience), the API is to APX (Application Programming Experience). In APX, it is important to answer the following questions:

- What should be exposed?

- What is the best way to expose the data?

- How should the API be adjusted and improved?

In addition, let's discuss why we should develop a nice Application Programming Experience.

A nice API will encourage the developers to use it and share it with others, creating a virtuous cycle where each additional successful implementation leads to more engagement and more contributions from developers who add value to your service. I'll start by saying that API design is hard.

Also, a nice API will help to grow an ecosystem of employees, customers, and partners who can use and help to continue to evolve your API in ways that are mutually beneficial.

There are four strategies for API design:

- Bolt-on strategy: This is when you have an existing application and add an API after the fact. This takes advantage of existing code and systems (Figure 4-1).

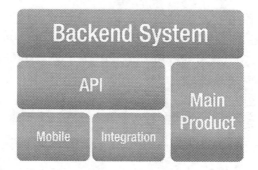

Figure 4-1. *Bolt-on strategy*

- Greenfield strategy: This is the other extreme. This is a strategy behind "API first" or "mobile first" and is the easiest scenario to develop an API. Since you're starting from scratch, you can make use of technologies and concepts that may not have been available before (Figure 4-2).

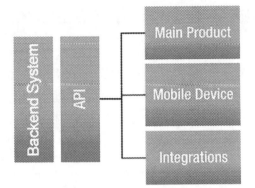

Figure 4-2. *Greenfield strategy*

A greenfield or API-first strategy is a simulation-based design implementation.

The simulation of a back-end system is the development of a back-end system without needing fully implemented back-end systems. With the simulation of APIs, consumers can start the development of apps without fully developed APIs.

- Agile design strategy: Agility is based on the premise that you can start without a full set of specs. You can always adapt and change the specs later, as you go and learn more. Through multiple iterations, architectural design can converge to the right solution. An agile approach should only be applied until the API is published.

- Finally, you have the façade strategy, which is the middle ground between greenfield and bolt-on. In this case, you can take advantage of existing business systems, yet shape them to what you prefer and need. This gives them the ability to keep working systems in place while making the underlying architecture better.

API Creation Process and Methodology

In this section, we are going to review the API creation process and methodology. In order to deliver great APIs, the design must be a first-order concern. Like optimizing for UX (user experience) has become a primary concern in UI development, also optimizing for APX (API user experience) should be a primary concern in API development.

Process

First, determine your business value. When thinking about business value, think of the "elevator pitch" about why you need an API. Developer engagement is not a great goal; you need a tangible goal: increase user engagement, move activity off the main product to the API, engage and retain partners, and so on.

Choose your metrics, for example:

- Number of developer keys in use

- Number of applications developed

- Number of users interacting via the API

- Number of partner integrations

- How the API is enhancing goals of the company as a whole rather than simply determining how many people have begun to integrate

API Methodology

It consists of five phases in the case of the agile strategy:

- Domain analysis or API description

- Architecture design

- Prototyping

- Building an API for production

- Publishing the API

Domain Analysis or API Description

Define your use cases for domain analysis. Who are the participants? Are they external or internal? Which API solutions do consumers want to build with the API? Which other API solutions would be possible with the API?

What would the API that the consumer wants to use look like? What apps does the consumer want to build? What data or domain objects does the consumer want to use in their app?

Break activities into steps or write down the usage scenario:

- A dependent resource cannot exist without another.

    - For example, the association of a podcast and its consumer cannot be determined unless the podcast and its consumer are created.

- An independent resource can exist without another.

    - For example, a podcast resource can exist without any dependency.

- An associative resource exists independently but still has some kind of relation, that is, it may be connected by reference.

    - As mentioned earlier

The next step is to identify possible transitions between resource states. Transitions between states provide an indicator of the HTTP method that needs to be supported. For the example of the podcast which could be added to a playlist, let's analyze different states (Table 4-1).

Table 4-1. *Domain analysis example*

State	Operation	Domain Object	Description
CREATE	POST	PODCAST	Creates podcast
READ	GET	PODCAST	Reads podcast
READ	GET/{podcast_id}	PODCAST	Reads podcast
UPDATE	PUT/{playlist_id}	PODCAST	Updates podcast

Also, verify by building a simple demo app. More than curl calls, this demo app provides a showcase for the API and can be reused in later stages.

Architecture Design

In this phase, the API description or analysis phase is further redefined. Architecture design should make decisions about

- Protocol
- Endpoints
- URI design
- Security
- Performance or availability

Detail design description:

- Resources

- Representations

- Content types

- Parameters

- HTTP methods

- HTTP status codes

- Consistent naming

In addition, look into reusability by looking at common APIs in the API portfolio. Design decisions should be consistent with the API in the API portfolio. The API portfolio is a collection of APIs in an enterprise, as discussed in Chapter 5.

As part of the design verification, the demo app can be further extended here with design decisions. Issues to be verified are that

- The API is still easy to use.

- The API is simple and supports use cases.

- The API follows an architectural style.

Prototyping

Prototyping is the preparation for the production implementation. Take complex use cases and implement end to end with high fidelity. The prototype is incomplete and uses shortcuts. It can have a simulation of the API if the back-end functionality is not available at the time of building the prototype. Once the prototype is made, then there is the acceptance test with pilot consumers as verification of the API. Pilot consumers are internal customers from the API provider's team.

Implementation

The implementation needs to conform to the API description and needs to be delivered as soon as possible. In addition, the API is fully integrated into the back-end system and API portfolio. This should have all the desired functionality as well as nonfunctional aspects of the API, like performance, security, and availability. At this stage, the API description should be stable since it has gone through multiple iterations. For verification, handpicked API consumers could be identified at this stage.

Publish

Publishing of the API does not require a lot of work, but this is a big milestone for the API. From an organizational perspective, the responsibility of the API is transferred from development to the operational unit. After publishing, there is no agility in the development process. Any change requires a traditional change management process. As part of the verification, there is analysis on successful vs. failed API calls and documentation gaps which are supported by the maintenance team.

API Modeling

Modeling the schema for your API means creating a design document that can be shared with other teams, customers, or executives. A schema model is a contract between your organization and the clients who will be using it. A schema model is essentially a contract describing what the API is, how it works, and exactly what the endpoints are going to be. Think of it as a map of the API, a user-readable description of each endpoint, which can be used to discuss the API before any code is written. Figure 4-3 shows the API Modeling framework where you have API specifications defined and generate API documentation. Also, generate server and client source code.

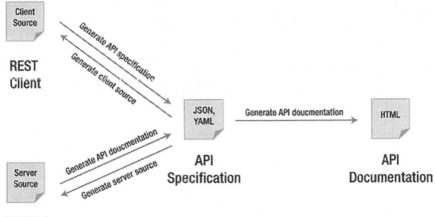

Figure 4-3. *API Modeling*

Creating this model before starting development helps you to ensure that the API you create will meet the needs described by the use cases you've identified. The three schema modeling systems and the markup languages they use are as follows:

- RAML: Markdown, relatively new. Good online modeling tool: RESTful APIs Modeling Language

- OpenAPI (Swagger): JSON, large community

- Blueprint: Markdown, low adoption

The OpenAPI (Swagger) exercise in this chapter shows the modeling done for the podcast resource.

Each of the schema modeling languages has tools available to automate testing or code creation based on the schema model you've created, but even without this functionality, the schema model helps you to have a solid understanding of the API before a single line of code is written.

Figure 4-4 shows the API Modeling tool.

Figure 4-4. API Modeling tool

Comparison of API Modeling

Table 4-2. Comparison of API Modeling tools

Category	Property	RAML	API Blueprint	Swagger
What is behind name?	Format	YAML	Markdown (MOSN)	JSON
	Available at	GitHub	GitHub	GitHub
	Sponsored by	MuleSoft	Apiary	SmartBear
	Initial Commit	Sep 2013	Apr 2013	Jul 2011
	Commercial Offering	Yes	Yes	Yes
How does it model REST?	Resources	X	X	X ("api")
	Methods/Actions	X ("methods")	X ("actions")	X ("operations")
	Query Parameters	X	X	X

(continued)

Table 4-2. (*continued*)

Category	Property	RAML	API Blueprint	Swagger
	Path/URL Parameters	X	X	X
	Representation	X	X	X
	Header Parameters	X	X	X
	Documentation	X	X	X
	References	`http://raml.org`	`https://apiblueprint.org`	`http://swagger.io`
	Design	API first	Design first	Existing API
	Code Generation	X		X
Who are the customers?				Apigee, Microsoft, PayPal

In summary

- Swagger has a very strong modeling language for defining exactly what's expected of the system—very useful for testing and creating coding stubs for a set of APIs.

- RAML is designed to support a design-first development flow and focuses on consistency.

- API Blueprint is more documentation focused, with user-readable models and documentation as its first priority.

Each project brings different strengths and weaknesses to the table, and in the end, it's really about what strengths you need and which weaknesses you cannot afford. Overall, RAML fared the best in these different categories, and, while the developer community is not as large as the others, I think it's safe to say it will keep growing.

The overall winner is RAML.

Best Practices

REST is an architectural style and not a strict standard; it allows for a lot of flexibility. Because of that flexibility and freedom of structure, there is also a big appetite for design best practices. These best practices are discussed here in this section.

Keep Your Base URL Simple and Intuitive

The base URL is the most important design affordance of your API. A simple and intuitive base URL design makes using your API easy. Affordance is a design property that communicates how something should be used without requiring documentation. A door handle's design should communicate whether you pull or push. For Web API design, there should be only two base URLs per resource. Let's model an API around a simple object or resource (a customer) and create a Web API for it. The first URL is for a collection; the second is for a specific element in the collection:

- `/customers`: Collection

- `/customers/1`: Specific element

Boiling it down to this level will also force the verbs out of your base URLs. Keep verbs out of your URLs as shown in Table 4-3.

Table 4-3. Nouns and verbs

Resource	POST Create	GET Read	PUT Update	DELETE Delete
/customers	New customer	List customers	Bulk update	Delete all
/ customers/12	–	Show customer 12	If exists, update If not, error	Delete customer 12

In summary

- Use two base URLs per resource. Keep verbs out of your base URLs. Use HTTP verbs to operate on the collections and elements.

- The level of abstraction depends on your scenario. You also want to expose a manageable number of resources.

  - Aim for concrete naming and to keep the number of resources between 12 and 24.

- An intuitive API uses plural rather than singular nouns and concrete rather than abstract nouns.

- Resources almost always have relationships to other resources. What's a simple way to express these relationships in a Web API? Let's look again at the API we modeled in nouns are good, verbs are bad—the API that interacts with our podcast resource. Remember, we had two base URLs: /podcasts and /podcasts/1234. We're using HTTP verbs to operate on the resources and collections. Our podcasts belong to customers. To get all the podcasts belonging to a specific customer or to create a new podcast for that customer, do a GET or a POST:

- GET /customers/5678/podcasts

- POST /customers/5678/podcasts

- Sweep complexity under the "?". Make it simple for developers to use the base URL by putting optional states and attributes behind the HTTP question mark. To get all customers in sfo city of ca state of usa country:

  - GET /customers?country=usa&state=ca&city=so

Error Handling

Many software developers, including myself, don't always like to think about exceptions and error handling, but it is a very important piece of the puzzle for any software developer and especially for API designers. Why is good error design especially important for API designers? From the perspective of the developer consuming your Web API, everything at the other side of that interface is a black box. Errors therefore become a key tool providing context and visibility into how to use an API. First, developers learn to write code through errors. The "test-first" concepts of the extreme programming model and the more recent "test-driven development" models represent a body of best practices that have evolved because this is such an important and natural way for developers to work. Second, in addition to when they're developing their applications, developers depend on well-designed errors at the critical times when they are troubleshooting and resolving issues after the applications they've built using your API are in the hands of their users.

Handling errors: Let's take a look at how three top APIs approach

- Facebook

  HTTP Status Code: 200

  ```
  {"type" : "OauthException", "message":"(#803) Some of
  the aliases you requested do not exist: foo.bar"}
  ```

- Twilio

  HTTP Status Code: 401

  ```
  {"status" : "401", "message":"Authenticate","code":
  20003, "more info": "http://www.twilio.com/docs/
  errors/20003"}
  ```

- Another example of error messaging from SimpleGeo

  HTTP Status Code: 401

  ```
  {"code" : 401, "message": "Authentication Required"}
  ```

When you boil it down, there are really only three outcomes in the interaction between an app and an API:

- Everything worked—success.

- The application did something wrong—client error.

- The API did something wrong—server error.

Error Code

Start by using the following three codes which should map to the three outcomes earlier. If you need more, add them. But you shouldn't need to go beyond:

- 200: OK

- 400: Bad Request

- 500: Internal Server Error

If you're not comfortable reducing all your error conditions to these three, try picking among these additional five:

- 201: Created

- 304: Not Modified

- 404: Not Found

- 401: Unauthorized

- 403: Forbidden

Check out this good Wikipedia entry for all HTTP status codes: https://en.wikipedia.org/wiki/List_of_HTTP_status_codes.

Versioning

Never release an API without a version.

- Make the version mandatory.

- Specify the version with a "v" prefix. Move it all the way to the left in the URL so that it has the highest scope (e.g., /v1/dogs).

- Use a simple ordinal number. Don't use the dot notation like v1.2, because it implies a granularity of versioning that doesn't work well with APIs—it's an interface, not an implementation. Stick with v1, v2, and so on.

- How many versions should you maintain? Maintain at least one version back.

- For how long should you maintain a version? Give developers at least one cycle to react before obsoleting a version.

- There is a strong school of thought about putting format (xml or json) and version in the header. Simple rules we follow: If it changes the logic you write to handle the response, put it in the URL so you can see it easily. If it doesn't change the logic for each response (like OAuth information), put it in the header.

Partial Response

Partial response allows you to give developers just the information they need. Take, for example, a request for a tweet on the Twitter API. You'll get much more than a typical Twitter app often needs, including the name of the person, the text of the tweet, a timestamp, how often the message was retweeted, and a lot of metadata. Let's look at how several leading APIs handle giving developers just what they need in responses, including Google, who pioneered the idea of partial response:

- LinkedIn

  `/people:(id,first-name,last-name,industry)`This request on a person returns the ID, first name, last name, and the industry

- Facebook

  `/joe.smith/friends?fields=id,name,picture`

- Google

  `?fields=title,media`

Google and Facebook have a similar approach, which works well. They each have an optional parameter called "fields" after which you put the names of fields you want to be returned. As you can see in this example, you can also put subobjects in responses to pull in other information from additional resources.

Pagination

Make it easy for developers to paginate objects in a database. Let's look at how Facebook, Twitter, and LinkedIn handle pagination. Facebook uses offset and limit. Twitter uses page and rpp (records per page). LinkedIn uses start and count semantically. Facebook and LinkedIn do the same thing, that is, the LinkedIn start and count.

To get records 50 through 75 from each system, you would use the following:

- Facebook: `offset` 50 and `limit` 2

- Twitter: `page` 3 and `rpp` 25 (records per page)

- LinkedIn: `start` 50 and `count` 25

Multiple Formats

We recommend that you support more than one format—that you push things out in one format and accept as many formats as necessary. You can usually automate the mapping from format to format. Here's what the syntax looks like for a few key APIs:

- Google Data: `?alt=json`

- Foursquare: `/venue.json`

- LinkedIn: `Accept: application/json`

API Façade

Use the façade pattern when you want to provide a simple interface to a complex subsystem. Subsystems often get more complex as they evolve.

Implementing an API façade pattern involves three basic steps:

1. Design the ideal API—design the URLs, request parameters and responses, headers, query parameters, and so on. The API design should be self-consistent. This means you give the developers the information they need.

2. Implement the design with data stubs. This allows application developers to use your API and give you feedback even before your API is connected to internal systems.

3. Mediate or integrate between the façade and the systems.

API Solution Architecture

Developers and architects often think of APIs as a continuation of the integration-based architectures that have long been in use within enterprise IT. But this is a narrow view.

To understand the demands and requirements on APIs, let's discuss typical solutions that are enabled by APIs.

Figure 4-5 shows the API solution architecture.

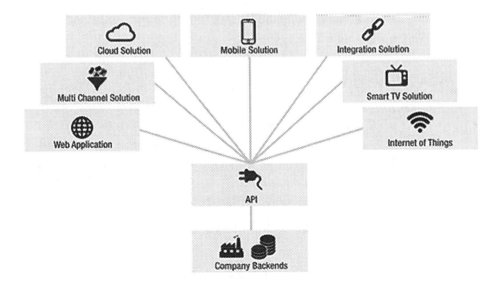

Figure 4-5. *API solution architecture*

API solutions typically consist of two components:

- Exposes the API

  - An exposed API resides on the server side, for example, in the cloud or on premise.

- Consumes the API

  - Web or mobile apps and embedded devices on IoT

Mobile Solutions

Mobile apps need to connect to the servers on the Internet to be usable at all or at least to be usable to their full potential—some business logic on the app and heavy-duty processing logic on servers in the cloud. Functionality hosted on these servers can be reached by API calls. Data captured on mobile devices is sent to servers by API calls, which hand the data to services and then to databases. Data delivered by APIs needs to be lightweight. This ensures APIs can be consumed by devices with limited processing power. Typically, the mobile app provider provides the APIs for the mobile app.

Cloud Solutions

SaaS cloud solutions typically consist of a web application and APIs. The web application is visible for the consumers. Under the hood, cloud solutions usually offer an API as well, for example, Dropbox, Salesforce, Workday, and Oracle Cloud.

Web Solutions

Web applications display dynamic web pages based upon user requests; web pages are created on the fly with data available from the back end. The web application pulls raw data from the APIs, processes the data (JSON, XML), and displays in HTML, for example, podcast or customer API.

Integration Solutions

APIs provide capabilities which are essential for connecting, extending the integrating software. By integrating software APIs, businesses can connect with other businesses. The business of an enterprise can be expanded by linking the business to a partner. Integration not only makes sense externally but also internally for integrating internal systems.

Multichannel Solutions

Today, an ecommerce system offers customers shopping on multiple platforms—mobile, web, tablet. It is required to provide a seamless experience when a consumer moves from one platform to another. This can be accomplished by providing a common API, which supports a multichannel maintaining state of user experience.

Smart TV Solutions

Smart TV offers not only TV channels, but provides interaction capabilities. These are all implemented by API calls to the servers.

Internet of Things

The Internet of Things is made up of physical devices with an Internet connection. The device connects to smart functions (e.g., sensors, scanners, etc.) which are exposed on the Internet via APIs.

Stakeholders in API Solutions

In API solutions, stakeholders are API providers, API consumers, and end users. We will discuss the roles of each here in this section.

API Providers

API providers develop, design, deploy, and manage APIs. API providers define the API portfolio, road map, and product mode. It is the responsibility of an API provider to decide which functionality is exposed by the API. In the solution-driven approach, only those APIs are built which are required by the consumer. In the top-down approach, API providers provide APIs which are good from an internal perspective, for example, from a reusability perspective.

API Consumers

Consumers need to know how to call an API and build an API client. API providers should provide a demo app to consume their API for the consumers.

End Users

End users do not call the API directly, but use the app developed by API consumers.

API Modeling

OpenAPI (Swagger)

MICRONAUT®
LAUNCH

Application Type	Java Version	Name	Base Package
Micronaut Application	11	flight	com.flight

Micronaut Version	Language	Build Tool	Test Framework
● 3.7.2	● Java	○ Gradle	● JUnit
○ 3.7.3-SNAPSHOT	○ Groovy	○ Gradle Kotlin	○ Spock
○ 2.5.13	○ Kotlin	● Maven	○ Kotest

+ FEATURES	⤴ DIFF	⌕ PREVIEW	🔧 GENERATE PR

Your Micronaut app is ready for takeoff.

Unix/Linux/macOS   Windows

Unzip the archive

```
unzip flight.zip
```

cd into the project

```
cd flight
```

Launch!

```
./mvnw mn:run
```

This tutorial walks you through the steps for creating OpenAPI specs using Swagger (Micronaut for a flight passenger API):

Import the flight folder in Visual Studio Code (VSC).

Create a model folder in VSC.

Create a controllers folder in VSC.

Create a service folder in VSC.

Create a Flight class in the model folder using VSC. Paste the following definition of the attributes of the Flight class and then select pasted code and using light bulb generate getter and setter methods.

Create a Passenger class in the model folder using VSC. Paste the passenger attributes' code and then generate getter and setter methods like for the flight object:

```
package com.rest.domain;
import io.swagger.v3.oas.annotations.media.Schema;
@Schema(description="Passenger")
public class Passenger {
 private String id;
 private String name;

 public String getId() {
       return id;
 }
 public void setId(String id) {
     this.id = id;
 }
 public String getName() {
       return name;
 }
 public void setName(String name) {
     this.name = name;
 }
}
```

Create a FlightService class in the service folder using VSC and paste the following folder. In this code, we are creating flightRepo for storing flights in memory. Get methods will be implemented to fetch details of a flight and list of all flights.

```
package com.rest.service;

import com.rest.domain.Flight;
import java.util.Map;
```

```java
import java.util.List;
import java.util.ArrayList;
import java.util.HashMap;
import java.util.concurrent.atomic.AtomicInteger;

public class FlightService {
static private Map<Integer, Flight> flightRepo = new
HashMap<Integer, Flight>();
static private AtomicInteger idCounter = new AtomicInteger();
public Flight getFlight(String id) {
    Flight flight = flightRepo.get(id);
    return flight;
}
public  List<Flight> getFlightsByPassenger(String
passengerId) {
    return new ArrayList<Flight>(flightRepo.values());
}
}
}
```

Create a PassengerService class in the service folder using VSC and paste the following code:

```java
package com.rest.service;

import com.rest.domain.Passenger;
import java.util.Map;
import java.util.List;
import java.util.ArrayList;
import java.util.HashMap;
import java.util.concurrent.atomic.AtomicInteger;

public class PassengerService {
static private Map<Integer, Passenger> passengerRepo = new
HashMap<Integer, Passenger>();
```

```
static private AtomicInteger idCounter = new AtomicInteger();
public Passenger getPassenger(int id) {
    Passenger passenger = passengerRepo.get(id);
    return passenger;
}
public  List<Passenger> getPassengers() {
    return new ArrayList<Passenger>(passengerRepo.values());
}
}
```

Create a FlightController class in the controller folder using VSC and paste the following code:

```
package com.rest.controller;

import com.rest.domain.Flight;
import com.rest.service.FlightService;
import io.micronaut.http.annotation.Get;
import io.micronaut.http.annotation.Controller;

import io.micronaut.http.HttpHeaders;
import io.micronaut.http.HttpResponse;
import io.micronaut.http.MediaType;
import io.micronaut.http.annotation.Produces;
import io.micronaut.http.annotation.Controller;
import io.micronaut.http.annotation.Delete;
import io.micronaut.http.annotation.Get;
import io.micronaut.http.annotation.Post;
import io.micronaut.http.annotation.Put;
import io.micronaut.http.annotation.Body;
import java.util.List;

@Controller("/flight")  // <2>
public class FlightController {
```

```
FlightService flightService;
public FlightController(FlightService flightService) { // <3>
    this.flightService = flightService;
}

 @Get("/{id}")
 public Flight getFlight(String id)     {
   Flight flight = flightService.getFlight(id);
   return flight;
 }
 @Get("/passenger/{id}")
 public List<Flight> getFlightsByPassenger(String id) {
    List<Flight> flights = flightService.
    getFlightsByPassenger(id);
    return flights;
 }
}
```

Create a PassengerController class in the controller folder using VSC and paste the following code:

```
package com.rest.controller;

import com.rest.domain.Passenger;
import com.rest.service.PassengerService;
import io.micronaut.http.annotation.Get;
import io.micronaut.http.annotation.Controller;

import io.micronaut.http.HttpHeaders;
import io.micronaut.http.HttpResponse;
import io.micronaut.http.MediaType;
import io.micronaut.http.annotation.Produces;
import io.micronaut.http.annotation.Controller;
```

```
import io.micronaut.http.annotation.Delete;
import io.micronaut.http.annotation.Get;
import io.micronaut.http.annotation.Post;
import io.micronaut.http.annotation.Put;
import io.micronaut.http.annotation.Body;
import java.util.List;

@Controller("/passenger")  // <2>
public class PassengerController {

  PassengerService passengerService;
  public PassengerController(PassengerService passengerService)
  { // <3>
      this.passengerService = passengerService;
  }

  @Get("/{id}")
  public Passenger getPassenger (int id)     {
    Passenger passenger = passengerService.getPassenger(id);
    return passenger;
  }
  @Get
  public List<Passenger> getPassengers() {
    List<Passenger> passengers = passengerService.
    getPassengers();
    return passengers;
  }
}
```

To get started, add Micronaut's openapi to the annotation processor scope of build configuration in the pom.xml file:

```
<path>
        <groupId>io.micronaut.openapi</groupId>
        <artifactId>micronaut-openapi</artifactId>
        <version>4.0.1</version>
</path>
```

For Swagger annotation, add the following to the pom.xml file:

```
<dependency>
    <groupId>io.swagger.core.v3</groupId>
    <artifactId>swagger-annotations</artifactId>
</dependency>
```

Once dependencies have been configured, the minimum requirement is to add the following to the Application class:

```
import io.swagger.v3.oas.annotations.OpenAPIDefinition;
import io.swagger.v3.oas.annotations.info.Contact;
import io.swagger.v3.oas.annotations.info.Info;
import io.swagger.v3.oas.annotations.info.License;

@OpenAPIDefinition(
        info = @Info(
                title = "Flight",
                version = "0.1",
                description = "Flight API",
                license = @License(name = "Apache 2.0", url =
                "https://foo.bar"),
                contact = @Contact(url = "https://gigantic-
                server.com", name = "Fred", email = "Fred@
                gigagantic-server.com")
        ))
```

Compile application using command "mvn package".

cd target/classes/META-INF/swagger

Generated OpenAPI YAML in file flight-0.1.yml.

Once you have modeled API, you can generate a document which could be shared with API consumers. Swagger allows to make API access in the browser and more readable. Next, we will configure Swagger.

Configure the following in the application.yml file to enable Swagger. You could find the application.yml file in the src/main/resources folder:

```
micronaut:
  router:
    static-resources:
      swagger:
        paths: classpath:META-INF/swagger
        mapping: /swagger/**
```

With the preceding configuration in place, when you run your application you can access your Swagger documentation at http:// localhost:8080/swagger/flight-0.1.yml.

Summary

In this chapter, we started with API design strategies and then looked into the API creation process and modeling. Best practices for REST API design are discussed, followed by the API solution architecture. We compared API Modeling tools and then developed an API for flight passenger using Micronaut.

CHAPTER 5

API Portfolio and Framework

Abstract

This chapter starts with the API portfolio architecture and then gets into the framework for API development. An overview of the API framework starting from the client to data is discussed, and then the focus is shifted to review the services layer with an exercise implementing the services layer.

API Portfolio Architecture

Usually, an organization does not have one API but several APIs. All the APIs in the portfolio need to be consistent with each other, reusable, discoverable, and customizable.

© Sanjay Patni 2023
S. Patni, *Pro RESTful APIs with Micronaut*, https://doi.org/10.1007/978-1-4842-9200-6_5

Requirements

API portfolio design is a concern for different API stakeholders. Both API consumers and producers have significant advantages over a properly designed API portfolio, and both parties formulate requirements for an API portfolio regarding consistency, reuse, customization, discoverability, and longevity.

Consistency

An API solution, such as a mobile app, may use several APIs from the portfolio, and the output of one API is the input of another. So consistency is required about data structures, representations, URIs, error messages, and behavior of the APIs. API consumers find it easier to work with if it behaves similar to the last one and delivers similar error messages.

Reuse

A consistent portfolio consists of many commonalities among the APIs. These commonalities can be factored out, shared, and reused. Reuse leads to a speedup in the development. By reusing common elements, the wheel is not reinvented each time an API is built. Instead, a common library of patterns and know-how is shared and reused. Reuse can be realized in several ways:

- Reuse of an API by several apps

- Reuse of an API by multiple APIs

- Reuse of parts of an API

APIs should not be developed for a specific consumer. APIs should always be used by several consumers, solutions, or projects.

Customization

There might be consumers who might have specific requirements from the APIs, if the consumers of APIs are not a homogenous group. In such a scenario, customizations are required to the APIs to meet a consumer's individual needs. This contradicts with reuse requirements, but both can be realized at the same time.

Discoverability

To expand the usage of APIs, it should be easy for the API consumer to find and discover all APIs in an API portfolio. An API portfolio design needs to ensure that APIs can be found and all the information necessary for proper usage is available.

Longevity

This means that important aspects of the API do not change and stay stable for a long time. What needs to be stable is the signature of the API, the client-facing interface. A change in signature will break the apps built by the API consumer. For example, with IoT on "h/w devices" it is not easy to change.

How Do We Enforce These Requirements— Governance?

An API initiative is often regarded as an innovation lab of an enterprise. Imposing governance can contradict innovation. So to manage these conflicting requirements, an API portfolio may be split in two portfolios. One portfolio is dedicated to innovation and experiment. This portfolio requires lightweight governance processes. Another portfolio is dedicated to stable, productive APIs, which are offered to external API consumers.

Consistency

Each enterprise may implement its own set of consistency rules. When consistency rules are defined, consistency checks can be realized as manual or automated. Lightweight consistency checks can be realized by manual quality checks or review by a colleague. A complementary approach is by automated code generation based upon API description.

Reuse

There are two types of building blocks that are offered by an API Platform like security, logging, and error handler. Any other functional commonality or reusable solution pattern can be realized as a composition of building blocks. You could have your "own" API or third-party APIs. Third-party APIs could be integrated in an API Platform by creating an API Proxy on its "own" platform. This helps the consumer with homogenous security. API Proxy and API Platform architectures are discussed in the next chapter.

Customization

An API consumer is interested in data formatting and data delivery. Data gathering is, however, no concern to the API consumer. So these could be separated into two parts: one API we call "utility API" covers the data gathering; the other API, which delivers data and formats to the consumer requirements, is called "consumer API." Utility APIs cannot be called directly by a consumer; only consumer APIs can call these.

Discoverability

This could be manual or automated. Manual: Discover by API catalog or yellow pages. Automated: SOAP based through UDDI and WSDL. REST: Limited with the OPTIONS verb of HTTP.

Change Management

From an innovation or business perspective, there are forces to publish APIs as early as possible. From an IT governance perspective, APIs are published as late as possible. In a compromise solution, APIs are published early but only to pilot consumers, with the expectation that there will be changes, and APIs will break the app. Changes are classified into three groups: backward compatible, forward compatible, and not compatible. Backward compatibility is given if the old client can interact with the new API (adding query, header, or form parameter as long as they are optional; adding new fields in JSON or XML as long as they are optional; adding endpoint, e.g., new REST resource; adding new operations to existing endpoints, e.g., in SOAP; adding optional fields to request interface; changing mandatory fields to optional fields in an existing API). Forward compatibility is given if a new client can interact with an old API. It's hard to achieve, and generally it is nice to have it.

- Incompatible changes: If a change in the API breaks the client, the change was incompatible.

- Removing: Renaming fields in data structures or parameters in a request or response.

- Changing URI: For example, hostname, port.

- Changing data structure: Making a field the child of some other. Adding a new mandatory field in a data structure.

API Framework

As we have discussed, there are multiple solutions to an API, for example, web applications, mobile applications, etc. Each of these solutions talks to an API which is implemented through a multilayered architecture using design patterns. A **design pattern** is a general reusable solution to a commonly occurring problem within a given context in software **design**. A **design pattern** is not a finished **design** that can be transformed directly into source or machine code.

As shown, the Figure 5-1 multilayer framework consists of the following:

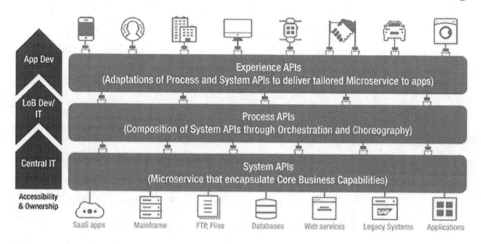

Figure 5-1. *API multilayered framework*

- Process APIs implemented by a services design pattern

- System APIs implemented by a data access object design pattern

- Experience APIs implemented by an API façade layer design pattern

Each layer is implemented using software engineering design patterns.

Process APIs: Services Layer

The services layer implements the business logic of the application: the reusable logic, process-specific logic, and the logic that interfaces with system APIs through orchestration and choreography. Orchestration (direct calls) in this sense is about aligning the line of business dev/IT request with the applications, data, and infrastructure. Choreography, in contrast, does not rely on a central coordinator. Rather, each API involved in the choreography knows exactly when to execute its operations and with whom to interact.

System APIs: Data Access Object

These system APIs or system-level services are in line with the concept of an autonomous service which has been designed with enough abstraction to hide the underlying systems of record, for example, databases, legacy systems, SaaS applications.

Typically, a data access object (DAO) is an object that provides an abstract interface to some type of database or other persistence mechanism. By mapping application calls to the persistence layer, DAO provides some specific data operations without exposing details of the system.

Experience APIs: API Façade

Both process and system APIs should be tailored and exposed to suit the needs of each business channel and digital touchpoint of solution architectures. The adaption is shaped by the desired digital experience and is what we call the experience API. This is implemented by API façade. The goal of an API façade pattern is to articulate internal systems and make them useful for the app developer providing a good APX (API experience).

Services Layer Implementation

The services layer implements the business logic of the application: the reusable logic, process-specific logic, and logic that interfaces with the legacy system. In the implementation of the services layer, a design pattern dependency injection is used. The general concept between dependency injections is called Inversion of Control. A class A has a dependency to class B if class A uses class B as a variable. If dependency injection is used, then the class B is given to class A via the constructor of the class A. This is then called "construction injection." If a setter is used, this is then called "setter injection."

A class should not configure itself but should be configured from outside. A design based on independent classes/components increases the reusability. A software design based on dependency injection is possible with standard Java. The Micronaut framework, which is used for the implementation in the exercises, just simplifies the use of dependency injection by providing a standard way of providing the configuration and by managing the reference to the created objects. The fundamental functionality provided by the Micronaut is dependency injection. Micronaut provides a lightweight container for dependency injection (DI). This container lets you inject required objects into other objects. This results in a design in which the Java classes are not hard-coupled.

FRAMEWORK: SERVICES

In the previous chapter, we implemented a flight passenger API for READ operations. This exercise uses a message domain object to implement CRUD (Create, Read, Update, and Delete) operations. The message domain object structure is pretty simple. There is an id, which identifies a message, and several other fields that we can see in the following JSON representation:

```
{ "id":1,
"message":"Welcome",
"from":"James",
"to":"John",
"creationDate":1388213547000
}
```

Pom.xml

Add the following to pom.xml:

```xml
<dependency>
    <groupId>javax.inject</groupId>
    <artifactId>javax.inject</artifactId>
    <version>1</version>
</dependency>
```

Message

Here is a POJO defining properties of the message:

```java
package com.rest.model;
public class Message {
 private int id;
 private String message;
 private String from;
 private String to;
 private String creationDate;

 public String getMessage() {
        return message;
 }
 public void setMessage(String message) {
     this.message = message;
 }
 public String getFrom() {
        return from;
 }
 public void setFrom(String from) {
     this.from = from;
 }
 public String getTo() {
        return to;
```

```
    }
    public void setTo(String to) {
        this.to = to;
    }
    public String getCreationDate() {
            return creationDate;
    }
    public void setCreationDate(String creationDate) {
        this.creationDate = creationDate;
    }
    public int getId() {
            return id;
    }
    public void setId(int id) {
        this.id = id;
    }
}
```

MessageController

In the message controller, we have CRUD operations for the message:

```
package com.rest.controller;

import com.rest.model.Message;
import com.rest.service.MessageService;
import io.micronaut.http.annotation.Get;
import io.micronaut.http.annotation.Controller;

import io.micronaut.http.HttpHeaders;
import io.micronaut.http.HttpResponse;
import io.micronaut.http.MediaType;
import io.micronaut.http.annotation.Produces;
import io.micronaut.http.annotation.Controller;
import io.micronaut.http.annotation.Delete;
import io.micronaut.http.annotation.Get;
```

```java
import io.micronaut.http.annotation.Post;
import io.micronaut.http.annotation.Put;
import io.micronaut.http.annotation.Body;
import java.util.List;

@Controller("/message")  // <2>
public class MessageController {

  MessageService messageService;
  public MessageController(MessageService messageService)
{ // <3>
      this.messageService = messageService;
  }
  @Produces(MediaType.TEXT_XML)
  @Get("/xml")
    public HttpResponse<?> messageXml() {
        Message message = new Message();
        message.setMessage("Hello from Micronaut");
        final String xml = encodeAsXml(message);
        return HttpResponse.ok(xml).contentType(MediaType.
        APPLICATION_XML_TYPE);
    }
  @Produces(MediaType.TEXT_JSON)
  @Get("/json")
    public Message messageJson() {
        Message message = new Message();
        message.setMessage("Hello from Micronaut");
        return message;
    }
    private String encodeAsXml(final Message message) {
        return String.format("<message>%s</message>", message.
        getMessage());
    }

    @Post
```

```
    public Message createMessage(@Body Message message) {
       messageService.createMessage(message);
       return message;
    }

  @Get("/{id}")
  public Message getMessage (int id)     {
    Message message = messageService.getMessage(id);
    return message;
  }
  @Get
  public List<Message> getMessages() {
     List<Message> messages = messageService.getMessages();
     return messages;
  }
  @Put("/{id}")
  public void updateMessage (int id, @Body Message update) {
     messageService.updateMessage(id, update);
  }
  @Delete("/{id}")
  public void deleteMessage(int id) {
     messageService.deleteMessage(id);
  }
}
```

MessageService

All the methods for CRUD (Create, Read, Update, and Delete) operations which
have operations in memory of messages are moved here:

```
package com.rest.service;

import com.rest.model.Message;
import java.util.Map;
import java.util.List;
```

```java
import java.util.ArrayList;
import java.util.HashMap;
import java.util.concurrent.atomic.AtomicInteger;
Import javax.inject.Singleton;
@Singleton
public class MessageService {
static private Map<Integer, Message> messageRepo = new
HashMap<Integer, Message>();
static private AtomicInteger idCounter = new AtomicInteger();
public Message getMessage(int id) {
        Message message = messageRepo.get(id);
        return message;
}
// add message
public void createMessage(Message message) {
        message.setId(idCounter.incrementAndGet());
        messageRepo.put(message.getId(), message);
}
// update message
public void updateMessage(int id, Message update) {
        Message current = messageRepo.get(id);
        current.setMessage(update.getMessage());
        current.setFrom(update.getFrom());
        current.setTo(update.getTo());
        current.setCreationDate(update.getCreationDate());
        messageRepo.put(current.getId(), current);
}
// Delete message
public void deleteMessage(int id) {
        Message current = messageRepo.remove(id);
}
public  List<Message> getMessages() {
   return new ArrayList<Message>(messageRepo.values());
}
```

API Tests(Curl)

```
curl -d '{ "id":1, "message":"test", "from":"test", "to":"test",
"creationDate":"12/12//2012" }' -H 'Content-Type: application/
json' http://localhost:8080/message

{"id":1,"message":"test","from":"test","to":"test","
creationDate":"12/12//2012"}
        curl -d '{ "id":2, "message":"test2", "from":"test",
        "to":"test", "creationDate":"12/12//2012" }' -H
        'Content-Type: application/json' http://localhost:
        8080/message

{"id":2,"message":"test2","from":"test","to":"test","creation
Date":"12/12//2012"}
 curl http://localhost:8080/message

[{"id":1,"message":"test","from":"test","to":"test",
"creationDate":"12/12//2012"},{"id":2,"message":"test2",
"from":"test","to":"test","creationDate":"12/12//2012}

curl http://localhost:8080/message/1

{"id":1,"message":"test","from":"test","to":"test",
"creationDate":"12/12//2012"}
                curl http://localhost:8080/message/2
{"id":2,"message":"test2","from":"test","to":"test",
"creationDate":"12/12//2012"}

curl -X "DELETE" http://localhost:8080/message/2

curl http://localhost:8080/message/2
{"message":"Not Found","_links":{"self":{"href":"/message/2",
"templated":false}},"_embedded":{"errors":[{"message":"Page Not
Found"}]}}
                        curl http://localhost:8080/message
[{"id":1,"message":"test","from":"test","to":"test",
"creationDate":"12/12//2012"}]
```

Summary

Now we have two APIs in our portfolio: one is for the messaging, and the other for flight passengers. The flight status API implements the relationship of two objects Flight and Passenger, whereas the message service allows the creation and deletion of messages in addition to read. It is important to follow the same design for both the APIs.

CHAPTER 6

API Platform and Data Handler

Abstract

This chapter starts with API Platform architecture and then gets into the data handler pattern for the integration of RESTful APIs with actual data sources within an enterprise to make it more meaningful to the consumers through APIs.

API Platform Architecture

API Platforms are used by API providers to realize APIs efficiently. We will review the following:

- Why do we need an API Platform?

- What is an API Platform?

- Which capabilities does an API Platform have?

- How is an API Platform organized? What is the architecture of the API Platform?

- How does the API architecture fit in the surrounding technical architecture of an enterprise?

© Sanjay Patni 2023
S. Patni, *Pro RESTful APIs with Micronaut*, https://doi.org/10.1007/978-1-4842-9200-6_6

Why Do We Need an API Platform?

It is certainly technically feasible to build APIs without any platform or framework. But why would you? For a moment, let's think about databases, which provide a platform for building applications. You could certainly build your application without a database and write your own data storage library. But we typically do not do that. We use an existing database as a platform. And this is the best practice for good reasons. It allows us to focus on building an application that serves the business case, because we can reuse existing, proven components and build the application quicker. The same augmentation applies to API Platforms: API Platforms allow us to focus on building APIs that consumers love, since we can reuse existing, proven API building blocks and build APIs quicker.

So What Is an API Platform?

An API Platform consists of one of the following three components:

- API development platform

    - It offers tools to design and develop APIs quicker.

    - It offers building blocks, which are proven, reusable, and configurable.

- API runtime platform

    - This primarily executes APIs.

    - It serves API responses for incoming API requests of the consumers with nonfunctional properties like high throughput and low latency.

- API engagement platform

  - This platform allows API providers to manage their interaction with API consumers. It offers API documentation, credentials, and rate plans for the consumers.

So Which Capabilities Does the API Platform Have?

The following are the capabilities offered by the three components of the API Platform.

API Development Platform

The API development platform offers a toolbox for API design and development targeted for API developers who work for API providers. The toolbox contains API building blocks, which are proven, reusable, and configurable. When building APIs, certain functionality is needed over and over again. This can be accomplished by building blocks. Building blocks can be reused. Building blocks are tested so bugs are not there, and these are configurable so they can be adopted for many purposes. The building blocks offered by the API development platform span the following features at the minimum:

- Processing of HTTP requests and responses

- Header

- Query

- HTTP: Status code

- Methods

- Security: IP-based access limitation, location-based access limitation, time-based access limitation, front-end authentication and authorization, OAuth, basic authorization, API key, back-end authentication and authorization (with LDAP, SAML)

- Front-end protocols: HTTP (REST), SOAP, RPC, RMI

- Data format transformation: XML to JSON and JSON to XML

- Structural transformation: XLST, XPATH

- Data integrity and protection: Encryption

- Routing to one or more back ends

- Aggregation of multiple APIs and/or multiple back ends

- Throttling to protect back-end rate limitation and throughput limitation

- Load balancing for incoming requests to the API Platform and outgoing requests to the back ends

- Hooks for logging

- Hooks for analytics

- Monetization capabilities

- Language for implementing APIs: Java, JavaScript, etc. (Jersey, Restlet, Spring)

- IDE for API development with editor, debugger, and deployment tools: Eclipse, JDeveloper, NetBeans

- Language for designing APIs: YAML, RAML, etc.

- Design tools for creating API interface designs: RAML, Swagger, Blueprint

- Tools for generating documentation and API code skeletons based upon design: RAML, Swagger

API Runtime Platform

The API runtime platform primarily executes APIs. It enables the APIs to accept incoming requests from API consumers and serve responses.

- It should deliver nonfunctional properties like

  - High availability, high security, high throughput

  - To meet these properties, the platform offers

    - Load balancing

    - Connection pooling

    - Caching

- It should also offer capabilities for monitoring of APIs, logging, and analytics to check desired nonfunctional properties are met.

API Engagement Platform

The API engagement platform is used by API providers to interact with its community of API consumers. API providers use the following capabilities of the API engagement platform:

- API management: Configuration and reconfiguration of APIs without the need for deployment

- API discovery: A mechanism for clients to obtain information about APIs

- Consumer onboarding: App key generation,
  API Console

- Community management: Blogs

- Documentation

- Version management

- Management of monetization and service-level SLAs

API consumers use the engagement platform for

- Overview of an API portfolio

- Documentation of APIs

- Possibility of trying APIs interactively

- Example source code for integration

  - Self-service to get access to APIs

  - Client tooling, such as code generation for clients

How Is an API Platform Organized? What Is the Architecture of the API Platform?

Usually, APIs are not only deployed on the production system, but need to be deployed on different stages of increasing maturity. The stages are also sometimes called environments. Each of the stages has a specific purpose and is separated from the other stages to isolate potential errors:

- Simulation: Used for playing with interface design,
  provides mocks or simulation of an API

- Development: Used for development, which will
  eventually go to production

- Testing: Used for manual black box testing and integration testing

- Preproduction: Used as a practice for production and for acceptance testing

- Production: Used as a real system for consumers

As shown in Figure 6-1, the API development platform is used for design and development. The API runtime platform is used for deployment. The API engagement platform is used for publishing the API.

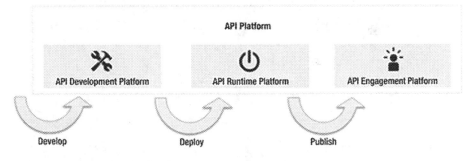

Figure 6-1. *API Platform architecture*

How Does the API Architecture Fit in the Surrounding Technical Architecture of an Enterprise?

An API Platform is not isolated, but it needs to be integrated in existing architecture in the enterprise. Firewall is used to improve security. Load balancers are used to improve performance and are usually placed between the Internet and the API Platform. IAM (Identity and Access Management) systems are for managing identity information and LDAP or Active Directory as shown in Figure 6-2.

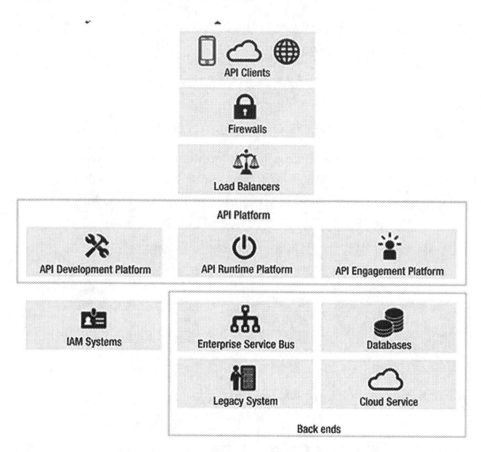

Figure 6-2. *API architecture in an enterprise*

Back-end systems for providing the core functionality of the enterprise: Back ends may be databases, applications, enterprise service buses, web services using SOAP, message queues, and REST services.

Data Handler

As mentioned in the previous section, we use an existing database as a platform. A data handler, a data access object (DAO), and a command query responsibility segregation (CQRS) all provide an abstract interface to some type of database or any other persistence mechanism. A data handler is a layer which handles data in the framework. A data access object is a design pattern used to implement the access from the database inside the data handler. The CQRS pattern, on the other hand, provides a mechanism to segment query and transactional data in the data handler.

Data Access Object

By mapping application calls to the persistence layer, a DAO provides some specific data operations without exposing details of the database. The advantage of using data access objects is the relative simplicity, and it provides separation between two important parts of an application that can but should not know anything about each other and which can be expected to evolve frequently and independently. Changing business logic can rely on the same DAO interface, while changes to persistence logic do not affect DAO clients as long as the interface remains correctly implemented. All details of storage are hidden from the rest of the application (see information hiding). Thus, possible changes to the persistence mechanism can be implemented by just modifying one DAO implementation while the rest of the application isn't affected. DAOs act as an intermediary between the application and the database. DAOs move data back and forth between objects and database records.

For accessing databases, there are different APIs available (e.g., JPA, which will be used in the class lab).

Command Query Responsibility Segregation (CQRS)

New demands are being put on IT organizations every day to deliver agile, high-performance integrated mobile and web applications. In the meantime, the technology landscape is getting complex every day with the advent of new technologies like REST, NoSQL, and the cloud, while existing technologies like SOAP and SQL still rule everyday work. Rather than taking a religious side of the debate, NoSQL can successfully coexist with SQL in this "polyglot" of data storage and formats. However, this integration also adds another layer of complexity both in architecture and implementation. We will talk about the following.

SQL Development Process

The application development life cycle means changes to the database schema first, followed by the bindings, then internal schema mapping, and finally the SOAP or JSON services, and eventually the client code. This all costs the project time and money. It also means that the "code" (pick your language here) and the business logic would also need to be modified to handle the changes to the model. Figure 6-3 shows the traditional CRUD architecture.

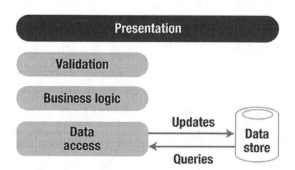

Figure 6-3. *Traditional CRUD architecture*

NoSQL Process

NoSQL is gaining supporters among many SQL shops for various reasons, including low cost, the ability to handle unstructured data, scalability, and performance. The first thing database folks notice is that there is no schema. These document-style storage engines can handle huge volumes of structured, semistructured, and unstructured data. The very nature of schemaless documents allows change to a document structure without having to go through the formal change management process (or data architect).

Do I Have to Choose Between SQL and NoSQL?

The bottom line is both have their place and are suited for certain types of data—SQL for structured data and NoSQL for unstructured data. NoSQL databases are more scalable than SQL databases. So why not have the capability to mix and match this data depending on the application? This can be done by creating a single REST API across both SQL and NoSQL databases.

Why a Single REST API?

The answer is simple—the new agile and mobile world demands this "mash-up" of data into a document-style JSON response.

Martin Fowler described the pattern called "CQRS" that is more relevant today in a "polyglot" of servers, data, services, and connections (Figure 6-4).

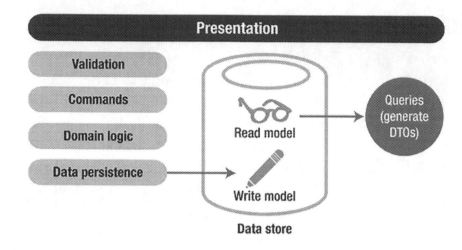

Figure 6-4. *Basic CQRS architecture*

In this design pattern, the REST API requests (GET) return documents from multiple sources (e.g., mash-ups). In the update process, the data is subject to business logic derivations, validations, event processing, and database transactions. This data may then be pushed back into the NoSQL using asynchronous events. The advantage of NoSQL databases over SQL for this purpose is that NoSQL has dynamic schema for unstructured data. Also, NoSQL databases are horizontally scalable, which means NoSQL databases are scaled by increasing the database servers in the pool of resources to reduce the load, whereas SQL databases are scaled by increasing horsepower of the server where the database is hosted. Figure 6-5 shows the CQRS architecture with separate read and write stores. When you have a requirement of very, very large data volumes, you would choose separate stores.

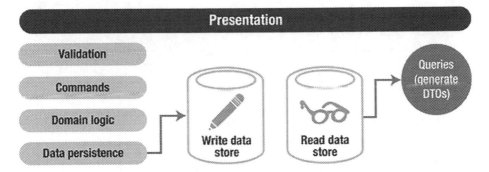

Figure 6-5. *CQRS architecture with separate read and write stores*

FRAMEWORK: DATA HANDLER

This exercise will implement a data handler or data access object for the quote domain object using the Java Persistence API (JPA). JPA is a Java specification for accessing, persisting, and managing data between Java objects/classes and a relational database. We will use our domain object message and implement CRUD operations using JPA in DAO.

Pom.xml

Update pom.xml with the following dependencies:

```
<?xml version="1.0" encoding="UTF-8"?>
<project xmlns="http://maven.apache.org/POM/4.0.0"
xmlns:xsi="http://www.w3.org/2001/XMLSchema-instance"
        xsi:schemaLocation="http://maven.apache.org/POM/4.0.0
http://maven.apache.org/xsd/maven-4.0.0.xsd">
  <modelVersion>4.0.0</modelVersion>
  <groupId>com.rest</groupId>
  <artifactId>quote</artifactId>
  <version>0.1</version>
  <packaging>${packaging}</packaging>
```

```xml
<parent>
  <groupId>io.micronaut</groupId>
  <artifactId>micronaut-parent</artifactId>
  <version>3.4.3</version>
</parent>

<properties>
  <packaging>jar</packaging>
  <jdk.version>11</jdk.version>
  <micronaut.version>3.4.3</micronaut.version>
  <micronaut.data.version>3.3.0</micronaut.data.version>
  <exec.mainClass>com.rest.Application</exec.mainClass>
  <micronaut.runtime>netty</micronaut.runtime>
</properties>

<repositories>
  <repository>
    <id>central</id>
    <url>https://repo.maven.apache.org/maven2</url>
  </repository>
</repositories>
<dependencies>
  <dependency>
    <groupId>io.micronaut</groupId>
    <artifactId>micronaut-inject</artifactId>
    <scope>compile</scope>
  </dependency>
  <dependency>
    <groupId>io.micronaut</groupId>
    <artifactId>micronaut-validation</artifactId>
    <scope>compile</scope>
  </dependency>
  <dependency>
```

```
      <groupId>org.junit.jupiter</groupId>
      <artifactId>junit-jupiter-api</artifactId>
      <scope>test</scope>
   </dependency>
   <dependency>
      <groupId>org.junit.jupiter</groupId>
      <artifactId>junit-jupiter-engine</artifactId>
      <scope>test</scope>
   </dependency>
   <dependency>
      <groupId>io.micronaut.test</groupId>
      <artifactId>micronaut-test-junit5</artifactId>
      <scope>test</scope>
   </dependency>
   <dependency>
      <groupId>io.micronaut</groupId>
      <artifactId>micronaut-http-client</artifactId>
      <scope>compile</scope>
   </dependency>
   <dependency>
      <groupId>io.micronaut</groupId>
      <artifactId>micronaut-http-server-netty</artifactId>
      <scope>compile</scope>
   </dependency>
   <dependency>
      <groupId>io.micronaut</groupId>
      <artifactId>micronaut-jackson-databind</artifactId>
      <scope>compile</scope>
   </dependency>
   <dependency>
<groupId>io.micronaut</groupId>
      <artifactId>micronaut-http-server-netty</artifactId>
      <scope>compile</scope>
   </dependency>
```

```xml
<dependency>
  <groupId>io.micronaut</groupId>
  <artifactId>micronaut-jackson-databind</artifactId>
  <scope>compile</scope>
</dependency>
<dependency>
  <groupId>io.micronaut</groupId>
  <artifactId>micronaut-runtime</artifactId>
  <scope>compile</scope>
</dependency>
<dependency>
  <groupId>io.micronaut.data</groupId>
  <artifactId>micronaut-data-jdbc</artifactId>
  <scope>compile</scope>
</dependency>
<dependency>
  <groupId>io.micronaut.reactor</groupId>
  <artifactId>micronaut-reactor</artifactId>
  <scope>compile</scope>
</dependency>
<dependency>
 <groupId>mysql</groupId>
 <artifactId>mysql-connector-java</artifactId>
</dependency>
<dependency>
  <groupId>io.micronaut.reactor</groupId>
  <artifactId>micronaut-reactor-http-client</artifactId>
  <scope>compile</scope>
</dependency>
<dependency>
  <groupId>io.micronaut.sql</groupId>
  <artifactId>micronaut-jdbc-hikari</artifactId>
  <scope>compile</scope>
</dependency>
```

```xml
  <dependency>
  <groupId>io.micronaut.data</groupId>
  <artifactId>micronaut-data-hibernate-jpa</artifactId>
  </dependency>
  <dependency>
  <groupId>io.micronaut.sql</groupId>
  <artifactId>micronaut-hibernate-jpa</artifactId>
  </dependency>
  <dependency>
  <groupId>io.swagger.core.v3</groupId>
  <artifactId>swagger-annotations</artifactId>
  </dependency>
  <dependency>
    <groupId>jakarta.annotation</groupId>
    <artifactId>jakarta.annotation-api</artifactId>
    <scope>compile</scope>
  </dependency>
  <dependency>
    <groupId>ch.qos.logback</groupId>
    <artifactId>logback-classic</artifactId>
    <scope>runtime</scope>
  </dependency>
  <dependency>
    <groupId>com.h2database</groupId>
    <artifactId>h2</artifactId>
    <scope>runtime</scope>
  </dependency>
  </dependencies>
<build>
  <plugins>
    <plugin>
      <groupId>io.micronaut.build</groupId>
      <artifactId>micronaut-maven-plugin</artifactId>
    </plugin>
```

```xml
<plugin>
  <groupId>org.apache.maven.plugins</groupId>
  <artifactId>maven-compiler-plugin</artifactId>
  <configuration>
    <!-- Uncomment to enable incremental compilation -->
    <!-- <useIncrementalCompilation>false</useIncremental
    Compilation> -->

    <annotationProcessorPaths combine.children="append">
      <path>
        <groupId>io.micronaut</groupId>
        <artifactId>micronaut-http-validation</artifactId>
        <version>${micronaut.version}</version>
      </path>
      <path>
        <groupId>io.micronaut.data</groupId>
        <artifactId>micronaut-data-processor</artifactId>
        <version>${micronaut.data.version}</version>
      </path>
    </annotationProcessorPaths>
    <compilerArgs>
      <arg>-Amicronaut.processing.group=com.rest</arg>
      <arg>-Amicronaut.processing.module=quote</arg>
    </compilerArgs>
  </configuration>
</plugin>
</plugins>
</build>

</project>
```

Product

Here is a POJO defining properties of a product or catalog:

```
package com.rest.domain;
import io.swagger.v3.oas.annotations.media.Schema;
import javax.persistence.*;
import javax.validation.constraints.Size;
@Schema(description="Product")
@Entity
public class Product {
 @Id
 @GeneratedValue(strategy = GenerationType.IDENTITY)
 @Column(name="ID")
 private Long id;

 @Column(name="NAME")
 @Size(max = 20)
 private String name;

 @Column(name="DESCRIPTION")
 @Size(max = 50)
 private String description;;

 @Column(name="CREATE_DATE")
 @Size(max = 40)
 private String createDate;;

 @Column(name="CHANGE_DATE")
 @Size(max = 40)
 private String changeDate;;

 @Column(name="UNIT_PRICE")
 @Size(max = 20)
 private float unitPrice;;
```

```
 @Column(name="CREATOR")
 private String creator;

public Long getId() {
    return id;
}

public void setId(Long id) {
    this.id = id;
}

public String getName() {
    return name;
}
public void setName(String name) {
    this.name = name;
}

public String getDescription() {
    return description;
}

public void setDescription(String description) {
    this.description = description;
}

public String getCreateDate() {
    return createDate;
}

public void setCreateDate(String createDate) {
    this.createDate = createDate;
}

public String getChangeDate() {
    return changeDate;
}
```

```
public void setChangeDate(String changeDate) {
    this.changeDate = changeDate;
}

public float getUnitPrice() {
    return unitPrice;
}

public void setUnitPrice(float unitPrice) {
    this.unitPrice = unitPrice;
}

public String getCreator() {
    return creator;
}

public void setCreator(String creator) {
    this.creator = creator;
};
}
```

Quote

Here is quote POJO having quote properties with mapping to quote lines:

```
package com.rest.domain;
import io.swagger.v3.oas.annotations.media.Schema;
import javax.persistence.*;
import javax.validation.constraints.Size;
import java.util.List;
@Schema(description="Quote")
@Entity
public class Quote {

 @Id
 @GeneratedValue(strategy = GenerationType.IDENTITY)
 @Column(name="ID")
 private Long id;
```

```java
    @Column(name="CUSTOMER_ID")
    private Long customerId;

    @Column(name="QUOTE_DATE")
    @Size(max = 50)
    private String quoteDate;;

    @Column(name="BILLING_ADDRESS")
    @Size(max = 20)
    private String billingAddress;

    @Column(name="BILLING_CITY")
    @Size(max = 20)
    private String billingCity;;

    @Column(name="BILLING_STATE")
    @Size(max = 20)
    private String billingState;;

    @Column(name="BILLING_COUNTRY")
    @Size(max = 20)
    private String billingCountry;;

    @Column(name="BILLING_POSTAL_CODE")
    @Size(max = 20)
    private String billingPostalCode;;

    @Column(name="TOTAL")
    @Size(max = 20)
    private float total;
    @OneToMany (fetch = FetchType.EAGER, cascade = CascadeType.ALL)
    @JoinTable(name = "Quote_Line_Mapping",
    joinColumns = @JoinColumn(name = "quote_id"),
    inverseJoinColumns = @JoinColumn(name = "id"))
    private List<QuoteLine> quoteLines;
```

```java
public void setQuoteLines(List<QuoteLine> quoteLines) {
    this.quoteLines = quoteLines;
}

public List<QuoteLine> getQuoteLines() {
    return quoteLines;
}

public Long getId() {
    return id;
}

public void setId(Long id) {
    this.id = id;
}

public Long getCustomerId() {
    return customerId;
}

public void setCustomerId(Long customerId) {
    this.customerId = customerId;
}

public String getQuoteDate() {
    return quoteDate;
}

public void setQuoteDate(String quoteDate) {
    this.quoteDate = quoteDate;
}

public String getBillingAddress() {
    return billingAddress;
}

public void setBillingAddress(String billingAddress) {
    this.billingAddress = billingAddress;
}
```

```java
public String getBillingCity() {
    return billingCity;
}

public void setBillingCity(String billingCity) {
    this.billingCity = billingCity;
}

public String getBillingState() {
    return billingState;
}

public void setBillingState(String billingState) {
    this.billingState = billingState;
}

public String getBillingCountry() {
    return billingCountry;
}

public void setBillingCountry(String billingCountry) {
    this.billingCountry = billingCountry;
}

public String getBillingPostalCode() {
    return billingPostalCode;
}

public void setBillingPostalCode(String billingPostalCode) {
    this.billingPostalCode = billingPostalCode;
}

public float getTotal() {
    return total;
}

public void setTotal(float total) {
    this.total = total;
};
```

QuoteLine

Here is quote line POJO with properties of the line item and mapping to the product:

```java
package com.rest.domain;
import io.swagger.v3.oas.annotations.media.Schema;
import javax.persistence.*;

@Schema(description="QuoteLine")
@Entity
public class QuoteLine {

 @Id
 @GeneratedValue(strategy = GenerationType.IDENTITY)
 @Column(name="ID")
 private Long id;

 @Column(name="QUOTE_ID")
 private Long quoteId;

@OneToOne(cascade = CascadeType.ALL)
@JoinColumn(name = "product_id", referencedColumnName = "id")
private Product product;

 @Column(name="UNIT_PRICE")
 private float unitPrice;

 @Column(name="QUANTITY")
 private Long  quantity;

public Product getProduct() {
    return product;
}

public void setProduct(Product product) {
    this.product = product;
}
```

```
public Long getId() {
    return id;
}

public void setId(Long id) {
    this.id = id;
}
public void setId(Long id) {
    this.id = id;
}

public Long getQuoteId() {
    return quoteId;
}

public void setQuoteId(Long quoteId) {
    this.quoteId = quoteId;
}

public float getUnitPrice() {
    return unitPrice;
}

public void setUnitPrice(float unitPrice) {
    this.unitPrice = unitPrice;
}

public Long getQuantity() {
    return quantity;
}

public void setQuantity(Long quantity) {
    this.quantity = quantity;
};

}
```

Next, we will create repositories for product, quote, and quote line items for CRUD operations.

ProductRepo

```
package com.rest.repository;

import io.micronaut.data.annotation.Repository;
import io.micronaut.data.repository.CrudRepository;

import com.rest.domain.Product;

@Repository
public interface ProductRepo extends
CrudRepository<Product, Long> {
}
```

QuoteRepo

```
package com.rest.repository;

import io.micronaut.data.annotation.Repository;
import io.micronaut.data.repository.CrudRepository;

import com.rest.domain.Quote;

@Repository
public interface QuoteRepo extends CrudRepository<Quote, Long> {
}
```

QuoteLineRepo

```
package com.rest.repository;

import io.micronaut.data.annotation.Repository;
import io.micronaut.data.repository.CrudRepository;
```

```
import com.rest.domain.QuoteLine;;

@Repository
public interface QuoteLineRepo extends
CrudRepository<QuoteLine, Long> {
}
```

Next, we will create a quote controller implementing Get, Post, Put, and Delete endpoints for the quote API.

QuoteController

```
package com.rest.controller;

import com.rest.domain.Quote;
import com.rest.repository.QuoteRepo;
import io.micronaut.http.annotation.Get;
import io.micronaut.http.annotation.Controller;
import io.micronaut.http.annotation.Delete;
import io.micronaut.http.annotation.Post;
import io.micronaut.http.annotation.Put;
import io.micronaut.http.annotation.Body;
import java.util.List;
import java.util.ArrayList;
@Controller("/quote")  // <2>
public class QuoteController {

  QuoteRepo quoteRepo;
  public QuoteController(QuoteRepo quoteRepo) { // <3>
      this.quoteRepo = quoteRepo;
  }
```

```
@Post
public Quote createQuote(@Body Quote quote) {
    return quoteRepo.save(quote);
}

@Get("/{id}")
public Quote getQuote (Long id)    {
   Quote quote = quoteRepo.findById(id).get();
   return quote;
 }
 @Get
 public List<Quote> getQuotes() {
    Iterable<Quote> quotes =  quoteRepo.findAll();
    List<Quote> result = new ArrayList<Quote>();
    quotes.forEach(result::add);
    return result;
 }
 @Put("/{id}")
 public void updateQuote (Long id, Quote update) {
    Quote quote = quoteRepo.findById(id).get();
    quoteRepo.delete(quote);
    quoteRepo.save(update);
 }
 @Delete("/{id}")
 public void deleteQuote(Long id) {
    Quote quote = quoteRepo.findById(id).get();
    quoteRepo.delete(quote);
 }

}
```

Creating quote

```
curl -d '{  "customerId":"123", "quoteDate":"11/07/2022",
"billingAddress":"722 Main St", "billingCity":"San
Jose", "billingState": "CA", "billingCountry":
"USA", "billingPostalCode": "95035", "total" :
123, "quoteLines" : [{"quoteId" : 1, "product" :
{"name":"test", "description":"test", "createDate":"test",
"changeDate":"12/12//2012", "unitPrice": 1.0, "creator": "creat"
}, "unitPrice": 12, "quantity" : 1}]}' -H 'Content-Type:
application/json' http://localhost:8080/quote
```

Reading quote

```
curl http://localhost:8080/quote/1
```

Summary

In this chapter, we started with the API Platform architecture and then got into the data handler pattern for the integration of RESTful APIs with actual data sources. In the exercise, we demonstrated the implementation of a data handler using JPA.

CHAPTER 7

API Management and CORS

Abstract

In this chapter, we will start with façade and review API management requirements/solutions available.

Façade

In this section, we will first review the façade design pattern, and then in the second part, we will get into details about how façade is applied to the APIs.

Façade Pattern

Before we discuss the façade pattern, let's consider what a façade is in the real world. The most obvious example is that of buildings, which all have an exterior to protect and decorate, hiding the internal workings of the interior. This exterior is the façade.

© Sanjay Patni 2023
S. Patni, *Pro RESTful APIs with Micronaut*, https://doi.org/10.1007/978-1-4842-9200-6_7

Now we can get closer to APIs by considering operating systems. Just like in buildings, an operating system provides an exterior shell to the interior functionality of a computer. This simplified interface makes an OS easier to use and protects the core from clumsy users.

This is where the definition of the façade pattern in On Design Patterns comes in handy:

> *Provide a unified interface to a set of interfaces in a subsystem. Façade defines a higher-level interface that makes the subsystem easier to use.*

Consider Figure 7-1; you can see how the façade pattern puts an intermediate layer between the packages of the application and any client that wants to interact with them.

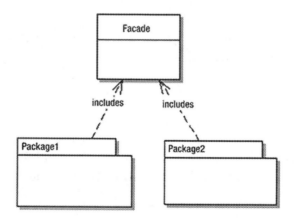

Figure 7-1. *Façade pattern*

API Façade

Like all implementations of the façade pattern, an API façade is a simple interface to a complex problem. Figure 7-2 shows internal subsystems in an enterprise. As shown, each internal subsystem is complex in itself: for example, JDBC hides the inner workings of database connectivity.

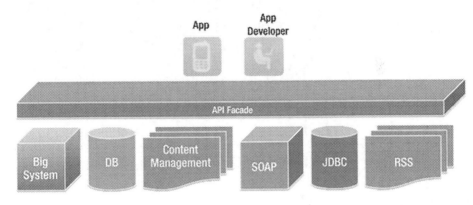

Figure 7-2. *Internal subsystems*

Figure 7-3 shows an API façade layer on the top of internal subsystems of the enterprise, providing a unified interface to apps.

Figure 7-3. *API Façade - High Level*

Implementing an API façade pattern involves three basic steps:

- Design the API: Identify the URLs, request parameters and responses, payloads, headers, query parameters, and so on.

- Implement the design with mock data. App developers can then test the API before the API is connected to internal subsystems, with all the complications that entail.

- Connect the façade with the internal systems to create the live API.

Figure 7-4 shows these layers.

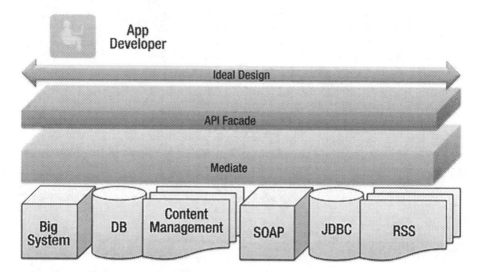

Figure 7-4. *API Façade-High Level*

API Management

An API management tool provides the means to expose your API to external developers in an easy and affordable manner.

Here are the features of an API management service:

- Documentation

- Analytics and statistics

- Deployment

- Developer engagement

- Sandbox environment

- Traffic management and caching abilities

- Security

- Availability

- Monetization

- API life cycle management

- API management vendors implement their solution in three different ways:

  - Proxy: All traffic goes through the API management tool, which is placed as a layer between the application and users.

  - Agents: These are plug-ins for servers. They do not intercept API calls like proxies.

  - Hybrid: This approach picks features of proxies and agents and integrates them. You can then pick which features you need.

API Life Cycle

The default API life cycle has the following stages:

- Analysis: The API is analyzed, and mock responses are created for a limited set of consumers to try out the API and provide feedback. It's also analyzed for monetization, as discussed in the following section.

- Being created/development: The API is being created: designed, developed, and secured. The API metadata is saved, but it is not visible yet nor deployed.

- Published/operations: The API is visible and eventually published and is now in the maintenance stage, where it is scaled and monitored.

In addition, there are two more stages:

- Deprecated: The API is still deployed (available at runtime to existing users), but is not visible to new users. An API is automatically deprecated when a new version is published.

- Retired: The API is unpublished and deleted.

These are discussed in the next section.

Figure 7-5 shows an API life cycle.

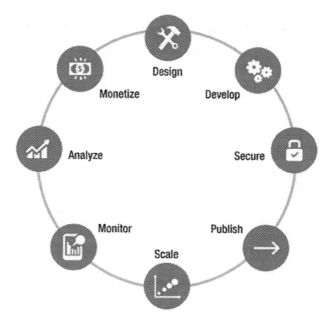

Figure 7-5. *API life cycle*

API Retirement

As old age comes, we get to retire, and the same is true with APIs. With time and due to the following reasons, an API is retired or deprecated:

- Lack of partner or third-party developer innovation

- Losing market share due to exposure of data by APIs

- Changes in the technology stack, for example, REST replacing SOAP

- Security concern: Making public APIs private due to security requirement of the information or data exposed by APIs

- Versioning: Most common reason due to functionality changes

Some of the examples of API retirement are Netflix, Google Earth, Twitter V1.0, etc.

API Monetization

Digital assets or services provide real value to customers, partners, and end users, and hence they should be a source of revenue for your company, as well as an important part of your business model.

There are three business models for monetizing APIs:

- The revenue share model, where the API consumer gets paid for the incremental business they trigger for the API provider.

- The fee-based model, where the API consumer pays the provider for API usage.

- The third and final business model is freemium. Freemium models can be based on a variety of factors such as volume, time, or some combination; they can be implemented as stand-alone or hybrid models (in conjunction with the revenue share or fee-based).

Cross-Origin Resource Sharing (CORS)

"Cross-Origin Resource Sharing" (CORS) is a mechanism that allows
TypeScript or JavaScript on a web page to make XMLHttpRequests to
another domain, not the domain the JavaScript originated from. Such
"cross-domain" requests would otherwise be forbidden by web browsers,
per the same origin security policy. CORS defines a way in which the
browser and the server can interact to determine whether or not to allow
the cross-origin request. It is more useful than only allowing same-origin
requests, but it is more secure than simply allowing all such cross-origin
requests. The Cross-Origin Resource Sharing standard works by adding
new HTTP headers that allow servers to describe the set of origins that are
permitted to read that information using a web browser.

How to implement CORS? For example:

```
return Response.ok() //200
.entity(quote)
.header("Access-Control-Allow-Origin", "*")
.header("Access-Control-Allow-Methods", "GET, POST,
DELETE, PUT").
allow("OPTIONS").build();
```

Summary

In this chapter, we reviewed API management requirements/solutions
and discussed Cross-Origin Resource Sharing (CORS) to support client
implementation.

Index

A

Agile design strategy, 53
Agility, 53
API consumers, 72, 80
API development platform, 98
   features, 99–101
   toolbox, 99
API engagement platform, 99,
      101, 102
API façade, 68, 69, 87, 128–130
API life cycle, 132
   analysis, 131
   being created/
      development, 131
   deprecated, 132
   published/operations, 131
   retired, 132
API management, 130, 131
API modeling, 58–61, 72
API monetization, 133
API multilayered framework
   API façade, 87
   components, 86
   data access object, 87
   services layer, 86
API platforms, 84
   API engagement, 101, 102
   API providers, 97

architecture, 97, 126
components, 98, 99
CQRS, 106
data access object, 105
data handler, 105
development platform, 99–101
importance, 98
NoSQL process, 107
organizations, 102, 103
SQL development
     process, 106
SQL *vs.* NoSQL process, 107
technical architecture, 103, 104
API portfolio, 57
   change management, 85
   consistency, 82, 84
   customization, 83, 84
   discoverability, 83, 84
   longevity, 83
   message, 25
   online flight, 24
   requirements, 82, 83
   reuse, 82, 84
API providers, 72, 97, 101
API Proxy, 84
API retirement, 132, 133
API Runtime Platform, 98, 101, 103
APIs implementation, 42, 44–48

© Sanjay Patni 2023
S. Patni, *Pro RESTful APIs with Micronaut*, https://doi.org/10.1007/978-1-4842-9200-6

V

Versioning, 66
Virtuous cycle, 52
Visual Studio Code,
        18, 27, 29

W

Web applications, 70, 85, 106
Web architectural style
    caching, 8, 9
    client-server, 7
    code on demand, 9

constraint and system
        property, 11
definition, 7
HATEOAS, 10
layered system, 8
stateless, 9
uniform resource interface, 8

X, Y, Z

XML and JSON formats, 41–49
XML comments, 33, 34
XML Schema, 33

Printed in the United States
by Baker & Taylor Publisher Services